Men-at-Arms • 333

Armies of Medieval Russia 750–1250

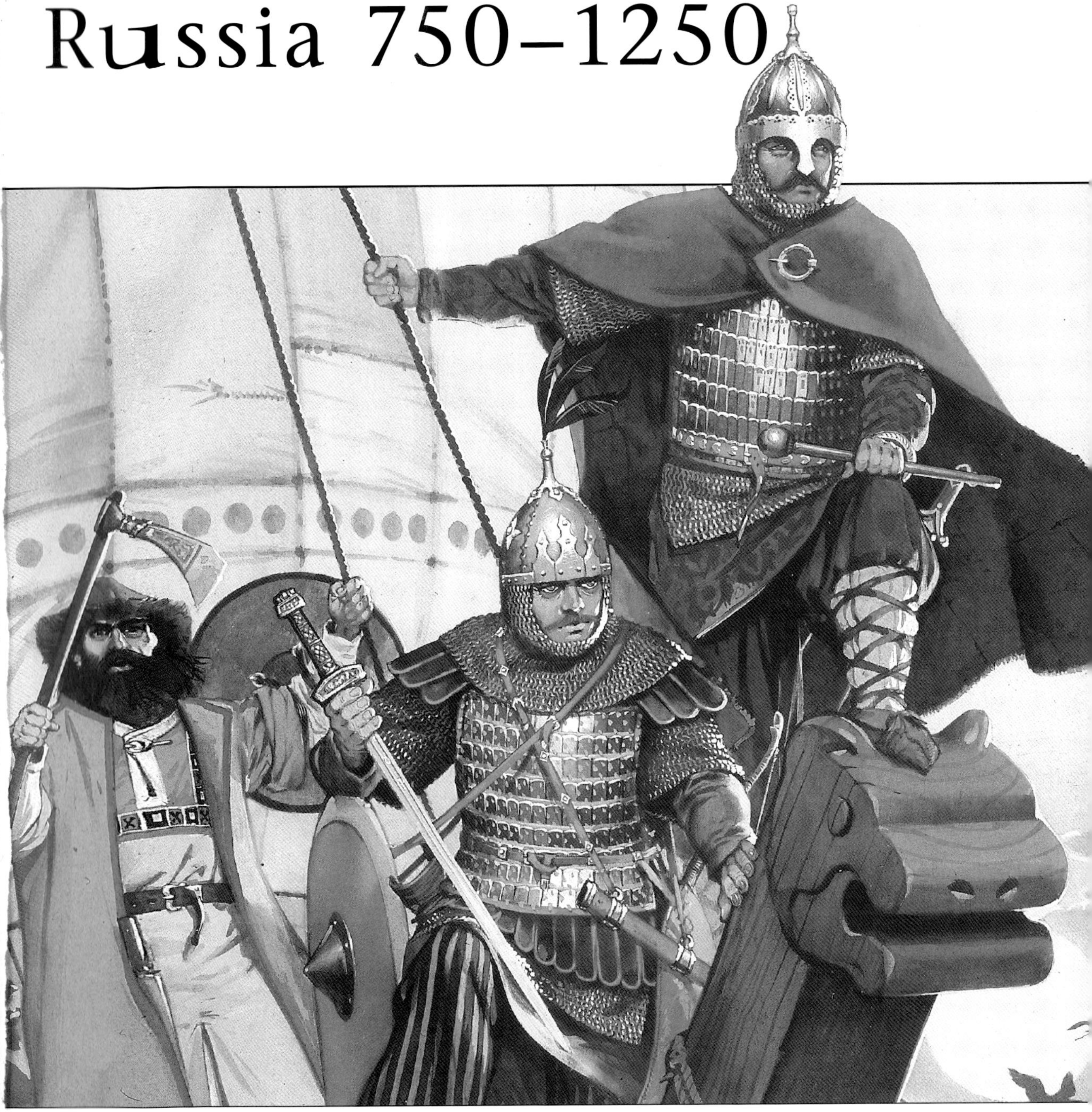

David Nicolle • Illustrated by Angus McBride
Series editor Martin Windrow

First published in Great Britain in 1999 by Osprey Publishing,
Elms Court, Chapel Way, Botley, Oxford OX2 9LP

Email: info@ospreypublishing.com

© 1999 Osprey Publishing Ltd.
Reprinted 2001, 2002, 2003, 2004 (twice)

All rights reserved. Apart from any fair dealing for the purpose of private study, research, criticism or review, as permitted under the Copyright, Designs and Patents Act, 1988, no part of this publication may be reproduced, stored in a retrieval system, or transmitted in any form or by any means, electronic, electrical, chemical, mechanical, optical, photocopying, recording or otherwise, without the prior written permission of the copyright owner. Enquiries should be addressed to the Publishers.

CIP Data for this publication is available from the British Library

ISBN 1 85532 848 8

Series Editor: MARTIN WINDROW
Editor: Martin Windrow
Design: Alan Hamp
Origination: Valhaven Ltd, Isleworth, UK
Printed in China through World Print Ltd.

For a catalogue of all books published by Osprey please contact:

NORTH AMERICA
Osprey Direct, 2427 Bond Street,
University Park, IL 60466, USA
E-mail: info@ospreydirectusa.com

ALL OTHER REGIONS
Osprey Direct UK, P.O. Box 140, Wellingborough,
Northants, NN8 2FA, UK
E-mail: info@ospreydirect.co.uk

www.ospreypublishing.com

Dedication

For Dr. Michael Gorelik, without whose encouragement this book would not have seen the light of day, and also for Galina and Gleb.

Artist's Note

Readers may care to note that the original paintings from which the colour plates in this book were prepared are available for private sale. All reproduction copyright whatsoever is retained by the Publishers. All enquiries should be addressed to:

Scorpio Gallery, PO Box 475, Hailsham, East Sussex BN27 2SL, UK

The Publishers regret that they can enter into no correspondence upon this matter.

ARMIES OF MEDIEVAL RUSSIA 750-1250

RUSSIA BEFORE THE RUS'

THE MEDIEVAL STATES of Rus' emerged within the forest and forest-steppe regions of what are now western Russia, Belarus and the Ukraine, while rival nomad states of the south were based upon the steppe. Both had towns, however, and it was the so-called 'nomad states' which were the more advanced throughout most of the Middle Ages. The entire region was criss-crossed by rivers and it was along their banks that most settlements grew up. Rivers provided the best arteries of communication, by boat in summer and as frozen highways in winter; not surprisingly, rivers also dominated warfare. These rivers effectively linked Scandinavia and western Europe to the Byzantine Empire and the world of Islam. Trade brought wealth and wealth attracted predators, both internal and external. In fact raiding, piracy and brigandage remained a major feature of medieval Russian history.

The steppe or *pole* featured prominently in Russian military history. It was an arena for heroic deeds, but also for military disaster. Much of it was dotted with woodland and marshes as well as being split up by rivers. At the same time the nomadic peoples, though no more warlike than their settled neighbours, had greater military potential and were more accustomed to tribal discipline. In the early Middle Ages the Slavs were relative newcomers who continued to colonize new territories even while medieval Rus' was being created.

Further north were the nomadic hunter-gathering peoples of the Arctic tundra, who do not seem to have had military or warrior aristocracies. One the other hand many Finnish or Ugrian tribes of the sub-Arctic *taiga* and northern forests clearly did have warrior elites. These tribes included the Est, Vod, Ves, Chud and Komi or Zyryans. The eastern Finno-Ugrian population had a more advanced culture and weaponry plus massive citadels made of earth and timber (see *Attila and the Nomad Hordes*, Osprey Elite series 30). They included the Merya, Muroma, Terjuhans, Karatays, Mari and Mordvians. Some were assimilated and disappeared during the 11th and 12th centuries, but others retain a separate identity to this day.

Then there were the Udmurts or Votyaks who, after separating from the Zyryans in the 8th century, were pushed eastwards by rival tribes to their final homeland along the upper reaches of the Vyatka and Kama rivers. The lands of the Khantz or Mansi of the *taiga* regions in the far north-east of European Russia were incorporated into the rapidly expanding Russian state of Novgorod in the late 12th century. Beyond the Ural mountains lived other Ugrian tribes, who seemed so terrifying that the Russians believed they had been locked behind a copper gate until Judgement Day.

Stone icon of St.George made in 1234 AD. Note the apparently lamellar cuirass, kite-shaped shield, and entwined foliate pattern on the lower border of the robe. (*In situ,* Cathedral of St.George, Yureve-Polskom)

3

Balt tribes related to modern Latvians and Lithuanians inhabited much of north-western Russia in the 8th century – perhaps sharing territory with newly-arrived Slavs, who moved in from the south and west. Other Baltic-speaking peoples were scattered across central Russia, the Goliad or Galindi not being 'Slavized' until the 12th century.

Descendants of those Iranian-speaking nomads who had dominated the western steppes before the Hun invasions of the 5th century still played a significant military role in various successor states in both the steppe and forest regions. For example, Alan military elites seem to have dominated several Slav tribes in southern Russia, and some of their military ceremonies were subsequently adopted by the Rus'. Along the shores of the Black Sea a number of originally Greek cities survived the upheavals of the early medieval era and remained centres of Greek culture. By the 9th and 10th centuries they also became centres of Jewish learning after part of the Khazar Turkish Khanate adopting Judaism. Even after the Khazars' collapse, Jewish communities continued to flourish in the Taman peninsula and as far away as Kiev. Meanwhile the Germanic Goths had come and gone, leaving Germanic words for weaponry and warfare in eastern Slav languages.

A large number of Magyars, ancestors of the modern Hungarians, still lived near the middle Volga river and were sometimes known as

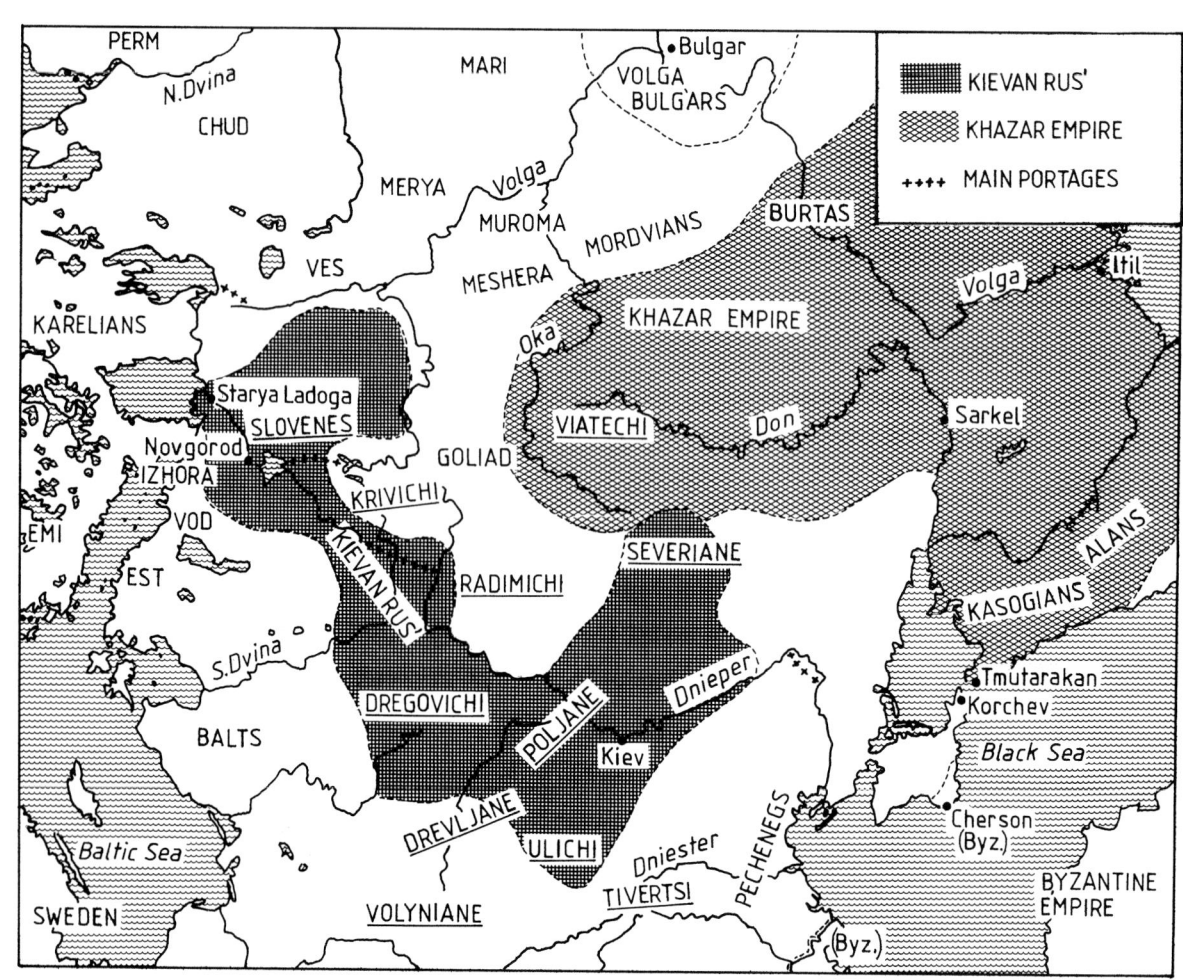

Russia and its peoples c.910 AD – note that to accomodate the north-south depth the map has been revolved so that north is to the left, south to the right, east to the top and west to the bottom.

White Ugrians. In fact the ruling elite of the Kiev region may have been Magyar allies of the sophisticated Khazar realm which dominated much of southern Russia. Subsequently they trekked westward to create the state of Hungary. Several Turco-Mongol peoples who had ruled the steppes south of the Russian forests left 'relic populations' in various areas (see again Elite 30). For example, the Black Bulgars survived between the Dnieper and Don rivers, while the Volga Bulgars had migrated northwards into forests west of the Ural mountains. There they established a rich trading state which remained a commercial rival of Russia until all were conquered by the Mongols in the 13th century.

Khazar drawing scratched on stone showing a horseman, from north-east of the Sea of Azov, 8th-9th centuries. Despite the crudity of the figure, some care has been taken to depict the high pommel and cantle of the saddle and the crupper and breast-strap of the harness; and note the flying ribbons or plumes behind the rider's head. (Hermitage Museum, St.Petersburg)

The Khazars had established a new capital at Itil where the mighty Volga flowed into the Caspian Sea while Kiev, future capital of the medieval Rus', probably still consisted of a fortified hilltop for Khazar tribute-gatherers. The Khazar army was also noted for armoured cavalry whose role would be inherited by the medieval Rus' military elite. West of the Khazars, and soon to sieze the steppes as the Khazars declined, were the Pechenegs. This largely pagan people remained a thorn in the side of Rus' for centuries until they in turn were ousted by the Kipchaks.

The Slavs

Thoughout these centuries steppe peoples stopped Slavs from expanding southwards. Instead Slavs clung to the forests, colonizing northward and eastward into areas inhabited by Balts and Finno-Ugrians. The Limit Antes who inhabited part of the Ukraine and lower Danube basin in the 6th century AD are, for example, sometimes called proto-Slavs. The little that is known about them suggests a patriarchal tribal society in which the status of women was notably low. This, and their reliance on blood vengeance as the foundation of a legal system, would remain characteristic of medieval Russia. Slavs steadily pressed northwards to reach Lakes Peipus and Ilmen by the 8th century, seemingly encouraged by the Avars who dominated vaste areas of eastern Europe until destroyed by Charlemagne around 800 AD.

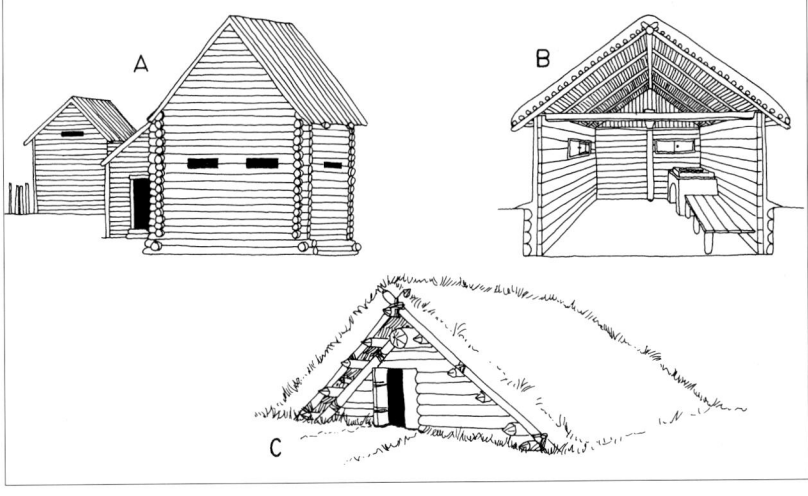

By the 9th century Slav settlements tended to be grouped along river banks for mutual defence and were often sited in forests or marshes. Although these people were farmers rather than warriors, their pagan pantheon was headed by Svarog, the 'god of white light', who may have been patron of weapons-making. Slav tribal names now appear: e.g. the Dregovichi, Krivichi and Slovenes inhabited the north-west and Novgorod

(A) Reconstruction of late pagan period buildings at Starya Ladoga (Starya Ladoga Historical Museum).
(B) Section through a reconstructed timber hall in the 8th-10th C fortified monastery of St.Novikh near Pereyaslavl, made of planks covered in earth-plaster (after Petrashenko).
(C) Reconstruction of a semi-subterranean 9th C house in Novotroitskoe (after Gimbutas).

Fortified hilltop near Izborsk known as Truvor's Stead, dated to the 8th-9th C; the name is a corruption of the Norse phrase *Treu Waer* meaning 'faithful warriors'.

**(A) Truvor's Stead (after Kostochkin).
(B) 11th-12th C fortifications of Southern Pereyaslavl (after Kirpitchnikov).
(C) Earthworks of 12th C town of Volokamsk (after Kostochkin).
(D) Earth ramparts of Gubino, 12th-13th C (after Kostochkin).**

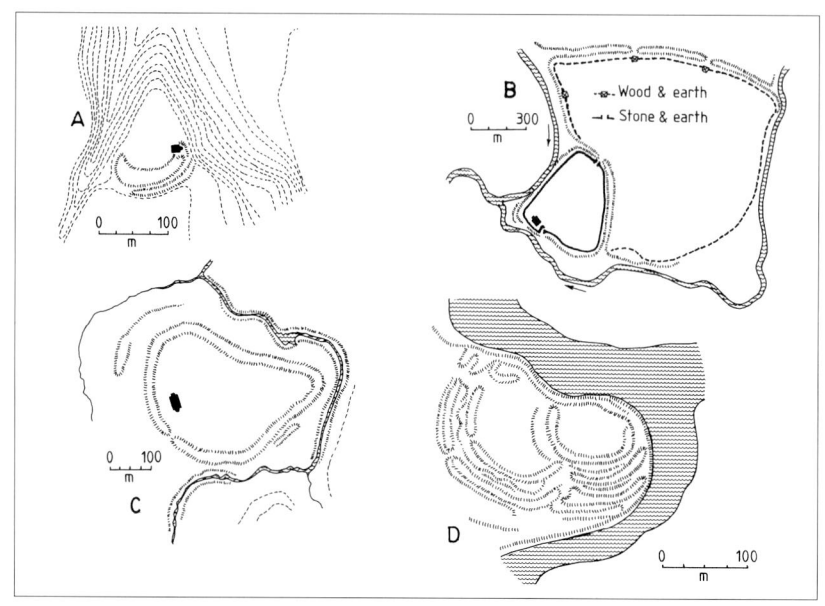

regions by the 11th century (in fact Slovenes may have built the first settlement at what became Novgorod). They also had cavalry, whereas most other Slav tribes fought almost entirely on foot.

In the south-west of what would become Russia the Tivertsi and Ulichi inhabited the upper reaches of the Bug river, where they defended themselves with large earth and timber fortifications. To the east, around Kiev on the river Dnieper, the most important Slav tribe were the Poljane. East of the Dnieper Slav forts became more abundant and stronger, some of them re-using long-abandoned Scythian earthworks. This was a dangerous but fertile frontier zone, often shared with steppe nomads who came in winter to graze their flocks. By the time the Scandinavian Rus' arrived in the 9th century the Poljane and some other Slav tribes were on the verge of establishing their own mini-states around several small towns. Each *rid* or clan had its own clearly defined locality and consisted of several *zadruga* – extended families. Tribal aristocracies existed, some of Alan origin, and these evolved into the *muzhi* 'notables' of medieval Rus'. Further east and north other Slav tribes pushed into Finno-Ugrain territory, defending newly colonized lands with earth ramparts topped by wooden stockades. Some were built by the Severiane tribe, while others are associated with the Viatechi.

Several eastern Slav groups, like those around Kiev, recognized Khazar overlordship as late as the mid-10th century, though excessive Khazar demands may have prompted other Slavs such as the Radimiche to migrate further north. This process of Slav expansion continued while the first real Rus' state was being formed along the rivers between Kiev and Novgorod. By the 11th century most former inhabitants had been assimilated. Nevertheless, differences amongst the eastern Slavs were still great, and there was as yet nothing which could be recognized as a Russian or even Ukrainian or Belarus people.

Meanwhile the old trade patterns between the Romano-Byzantine and Sassanian-Iranian empires

Carvings of huntsmen on foot with bow and spear, dated to 1193-97; others in the same series show hunters on horseback. (*In situ* Cathedral of Dimitri Sobor, Vladimir; author's photographs)

had collapsed in the 7th century, only to be replaced by an even richer and more extensive trade network from the mid-8th century onwards. A new economic powerhouse had developed in the Middle East, centred upon the capital of the 'Abbasid Caliphs at Baghdad and fuelled by free circulation of gold and silver Islamic coinage. Nothing like it had been seen before, and it attracted merchants from China, India, Western Europe, the British Isles and Scandinavia. It was the lure of 'Silverland' – as the Scandinavians called Islamic regions of the Middle East – which drew Scandinavian raiders as well as traders along the rivers of Russia, searching for the source of all that wealth. A new chapter was about to begin in the history of the eastern Slavs.

CHRONOLOGY

c.750	Scandinavian settlement at Starya Ladoga.
c.838	Emergence of a Rus' 'state' under a *Khagan*.
854-56	Possible arrival of 'Prince' Rurik from Scandinavia.
c.858	Rurik takes area around Kiev from previous Magyar-Khazar rulers.
860	First Rus' attack on Byzantine Constantinople.
864-83	Rus' raids against Islamic regions around Caspian Sea.
c.868	Rus' possibly take control of town of Kiev.
907-13	Rus' campaigns against Byzantine Empire and Islamic world.
c.930	Khagan Igor of the Volga Rus' takes control of Kiev.
c.965	Rus' devastate Khazar capital of Itil, raid Islamic areas, win access to Black Sea, attack Volga Bulgars in attempt to control eastern trade routes.
980-82	Vladimir Sviatoslavich become Prince of Kiev, crushes Slav tribal risings.
988	Prince Vladimir converts Rus' to Orthodox Christianity.
990-1015	Intermittent warfare between Rus' and Pechenegs.
1016-24	Civil wars between princes for throne of Kiev.
1032	Novgorod sends expedition to 'Iron Gates' in the far northeast, probably meaning Pechora river or beyond.
1042-43	Treaty between Rus' and Poland; war between Rus' and Byzantium.
1055	First appearance of Kipchaks on western steppes.
1061-62	Kipchaks raid Rus' territory.
1064	War between Kiev and Poland.
1068-69	Kipchaks defeat Rus' armies at river Alta; Prince Sviatoslav defeats Kipchak raid near Chernigov.
1077	Prince Volodimir Monomax of Pereyaslavl is first to employ *Chernye Klobuki* auxiliaries against fellow princes.
1079	Disappearance of military expedition to the river Ob.
1097	Conference of princes at Liubech regularizes system of inheritance of principalities and throne of Kiev.
1103-16	Rus' defeat Kipchaks and destroy Kipchak tribes in northern Donets.
1120	Rus' attack Volga Bulgars.
1132-34	Rus' civil war.
1136	Novgorod accepts no further rulers appointed by Kiev.

Wall painting of a huntsman fighting a bear. (*In situ* Cathedral of Santa Sofia, Kiev)

1148-9	Minor conflicts between Novgorod and Iaroslavl'-Suzdal.
1164	Prince of Vladimir invades Volga Bulgars.
1169	Prince of Vladimir sacks Kiev during civil war.
1171	Kipchak tribes united under Könchak Khan.
1183	Rus' attack Volga Bulgars, Kipchaks and Mordvians.
1185	Prince Igor of Novgorod-Seversk attacks Kipchaks but is defeated (origins of *Prince Igor* epic).
1193	Army sent by Novgorod to punish Pechora and Ugrians almost wiped out.
1199-1205	Civil war for throne of Grand Prince of Kiev.
1206	River fleet sent to reassert Rus' hegemony over Lett and Liv tribes is defeated by German garrison.
1216	Civil war between Rus' princes culminates at battle of Lipitsa.
1218-20	Suzdal attacks Volga Bulgars; Prince Mstislav of Novgorod retakes Galich from Hungarians with help of Kipchaks under Köten Khan.
1223	First Mongol invasion of western steppes defeats Rus' princes and Kipchaks at River Kalka.
1229	Mongols attack Saksin, Volga Bulgars and Kipchaks.
1230	Combined armies of Suzdal, Riazan and Murom ravage Mordvian territory.
1231	Rus' civil war for throne of Kiev.
1236	Mongols destroy Volga Bulgar cities.
1237-39	Mongols invade Rus' territory, conquer Vladimir, defeat northern princes at battle of Sit', conquer Chernigov.
1240	Prince Alexander defeats Swedish invaders on river Neva; Mongols conquer Kiev.
1242	Prince Alexander Nevski defeats German Crusade on Lake Peipus.
1243-46	Mongol Great Khan confirms certain Rus' princes in their positions.
1248-49	Rus' princes in civil war for throne of Vladimir; Andrei

	confirmed in possession of Vladimir by Mongol Great Khan, then forms anti-Mongol alliance with Daniil of Volhynia-Galich.
1252	Princes Andrei and Daniil defeated by Mongols.
1253-4	Orthodox Church in Volhynia-Galich accepts Papal authority; Mindaugas of Lithuania and Daniil of Volhynia-Galich establish anti-Mongol alliance; failure of Western powers to help causes Prince Daniil to make terms with Mongols.
1257-59	Mongols enforce census of population in most Rus' principalities.

PAGAN RUS'

From the 8th to 10th centuries the only towns in eastern Europe were trading settlements, where Scandinavian merchants were only one group amongst many. These Scandinavians could also be seen as 'nomads of the seas and rivers', just at Turco-Mongols were 'nomads of the steppes'. Their earliest presence in Russia is recorded in later legends, though archaeology can throw additional light. Only in the later 8th century did these newcomers start to dominate the local population. Scandinavians also ousted the *Radaniya* Jewish merchants who had previously dominated eastern European trade. As a result men from Sweden were a powerful presence between the Baltic and Black Seas and along the Volga river long before the semi-legendary figure of Rurik arrived. Their leaders were known by the Turkish title of *Khagans*.

But who were these Rus' who established the first Russian state? Were they Scandinavians, or did they include other Europeans or indigenous Slavs; and what part did Turks, Finno-Ugrians or Iranians play? The first references to the Rus' appear in the 9th century, and they seem to have been more willing to use violence than earlier traders had been. Three major settlements were created or taken over in northern Russia: Old Ladoga, known to Scandinavians as Aldegjuborg; Gorodische, which remained the main northern trading and perhaps political centre until the 10th century; and Novgorod, which the Scandinavians called Holmgarthr. Of these Novgorod was the best sited for trade and eventually superceded the others. It overlooked the Volkhov, which formed a vital link in a chain of rivers from the Baltic to Kiev and on towards Constantinople, as well as – via the Volga and Caspian Sea – to the Islamic world.

The second centre of the *Khagans* of Rus' was around

Aerial view of the site of the 12th century fortified settlement of Mikulin. (APN photo)

Iaroslavl near the upper Volga river; but here their history is less clear. Nevertheless, they were clearly trading and raiding down the Volga to the Caspian and the Islamic Caucasus by the 9th century. They had no wish to challenge the Volga Bulgars militarily, and the few defensive structures they built faced a threat from other Rus' to the west.

The third centre of Rus' power arose in the second half of the 9th century. As the power of eastern Islamic lands declined, that of the Byzantine Empire revived. This made trade with Byzantium more attractive, the most obvious route being down the Dnieper river and across the Black Sea. Though the Khazars continued to dominate areas east of the Dnieper well into the 10th century, the Rus' won acceptance from the Slavs around Kiev by demanding less tribute. Civil wars also weakened the Khazars and probably enabled a leading Rus' clan to be recognized as local *Khagans* by 839 AD, with several centres of power including Starya Ladoga, Gorodische and perhaps the Starskii Fort on the upper Volga.

Rurik, Igor, and the Khazar decline

According to legend, a Scandinavian nobleman named Rurik was invited to the Novgorod area in 862. Some scholars have identified him as Roric of Jutland, a Danish warlord mentioned in western sources. In reality Rurik probably arrived almost twenty years earlier, after which he and his followers spread their authority southward along the Dvina and Dnieper rivers, driving out or incorporating the previous Swedish Rus' merchant-adventurers. A generation later a large part of those Magyars who had dominated the Kiev area migrated westward into what is now Hungary, though whether they were pushed by Bulgarians, Pechenegs, Rus' or all three remains unclear.

The Rus' may not yet have been a major military power, but they and their local supporters built large river fleets, sent them thousands of miles to raid or trade, and also controlled strategic portages between major rivers. In fact the hard-pressed Khazars probably agreed to a Rus' takeover if the latter continued to recognize Khazar overlordship. Finally, around 930 AD, the Rus' leader Igor took formal control of Kiev which soon became the main centre of Rus' power. Within a few decades Igor of Kiev was recognized as a hereditary prince who, with his *Druzhina* armed following, made annual *poliudie* tribute-gathering journeys around his amorphous realm. A recognizable 'state' was clearly in the making.

The most reliable descriptions of the early Rus' are found in Arabic sources. Rus' society was clearly very Scandinavian in its appearance, attitudes and beliefs, while the *Khagan* was largely a figurehead reliant

Reconstruction of Mstislav as it would have appeared in the 12th century. (APN)

on 400 warrior companions. The name *Varjazi* or, in Byzantine Greek, *Varangians* was sometimes given to the warrior elite of this new Kievan Rus', but in fact the *Varjazi* were a separate group of Scandinavian adventurers, who included many pagans at a time when Christianity was spreading across Scandinavia itself. Some travelled in large groups like ready-made armies led by Swedish, Norwegian or Danish noblemen. The *Varjazi* also formed warlike brotherhoods, who were not only expensive to hire but were often in a position to demand prompt payment. One *Varjazi* army was hired by Vladimir of Kiev while he was exiled in Scandinavia. He used them to take the Kievan throne, but then wisely shipped most of them off to the Byzantine emperor. Other Rus' mercenaries who served the Khazars in the early 10th century may have been *Varjazi-Varangians* as, perhaps, were those seen in Muslim-ruled Georgia and Armenia.

It would, however, be wrong to see the creation of Kievan Rus' solely as a Scandinavian venture. Existing Slav tribal elites were involved, so that by the time of Vladimir the warrior and merchant aristocracies of Kiev were a mixture of Scandinavian and Slav families. In fact the power of the *Khagans* depended upon an alliance of interests between the ruler, his largely Scandinavian *Druzhina*, and the urban merchants – who were themselves of mixed origins. Ex-Khazar tribal groups played a key role in administration and the army, since their culture was more advanced than that of the Scandinavian Rus'. Meanwhile Balts and Finns retained their own social and perhaps military structure under the distant overlordship of Kiev.

Nor were the Rus' merely warriors. They switched easily between raiding and trading, depending on what seemed more profitable. From 860 onwards they even challenged the might of Byzantium, though the first attacks on the Byzantine Empire may have been undertaken without the *Khagan's* official agreement. The same might have been true of Rus' raids against the wealthy Islamic south-western coasts of the Caspian Sea. As a result the Byzantine, Khazar and

Remains of the earth ramparts around the Suzdal Kremlin today. (Author's photograph)

Model of the Suzdal Kremlin as it would have appeared in the 11th-13th centuries. Note the impressive size of the earth rampart, topped with a substantial timber wall complete with towers at intervals. (Historical Museum, Suzdal)

Russia and its peoples c.1180 AD (normal orientation, with north at top).

Islamic states started to take the warlike Rus' seriously, and sent official embassies to Kiev. As an early 10th century Islamic geographer wrote: *'The Rus are strong and vigilant, and their raids are not made on horseback but they raid and go to war only in ships.'* By bribing or threatening their way past Khazar garrisons at the mouth of the Volga, Rus' adventurers brought naval warfare to the Caspian Sea for the first time. Nevertheless, the pickings were not always easy, and even the enfeebled Khazars could defeat Rus' raiders on their home ground in 941 AD.

Such raids sometimes had a clear strategic purpose. In the 960s, for example, a series of ambitious Rus' expeditions were intended to win control of the entire trade network across eastern Slav lands and the western steppes. The result was a disaster, even for the Rus', since none of the competing successor states could impose peace upon the steppes as the Khazars had done. The Rus' lost what control they enjoyed over the western steppes, where fierce Pechenegs nomads were far more inclined to attack the Rus' than the Khazars had been. This was doubly unfortunate, because trade with Byzantium was increasing and the route to Constantinople lay along rivers which ran through Pecheneg territory. Here travellers either paid the nomads' transit fees or had to fight their way through.

By 944 the Rus' had established outposts where the main rivers flowed into the Black Sea. The most important were at the mouth of the Dnieper, where Rus' ships wintered while their crews rested – though this worried the Byzantines, who insisted that the Rus' erect no permanent fortifications. An alternative strategy was to form an alliance with the Pechenegs against the Byzantine Empire. This was attempted in 971-2 when Sviatoslav tried to establish a new capital on the lower Danube river by invading both Bulgaria and Byzantium. He failed, and was killed on his way home by his erstwhile Pecheneg allies.

Reconstruction of the gate of a large 11th-12th century fortified town. (APN)

Rus' warfare

In Byzantine eyes the armies which fought these far-ranging campaigns were not impressive. According to Photios, one was *'an unofficered army, equipped in servile fashion... nomadic... leaderless'*. This was an exaggeration, as the early Rus' did have a rudimentary command structure. Their armies consisted of three parts: the ruler's own *Druzhina* or armed household, mercenary *Varjazi*, and assorted tribal levies. Armies also differed according to the campaign; the army which Sviatoslav led to the Danube was not like those sent against the Khazars. In the Balkans the Rus' largely fought as infantry, with cavalry supplied by steppe or Hungarian allies. During steppe campaigns most troops travelled by river and fought on foot, though many Rus' were already mounted. The development of Rus' cavalry was a major feature of the 10th century and, not surprisingly, most techniques were learned from the nomads.

Another feature of 10th century Rus' warfare was its extreme brutality, the Rus' and *Varjazi* horrifying Byzantines and Muslims by their use of terror. Ritual combat was another feature of early Rus' society which continued into the Christian period. Vengeance and blood-money remained central to the later *Russkaya Pravda* legal code, which stated that: *'If a man kills a man, let him be avenged by his brother or father or son or nephew. If there is no one to avenge him, let the price on his head be seventy grivnas if he be a prince's man or a prince's Druzhina's man. If he be a Rus' or loyal supporter or merchant or nobleman's Druzhina or swordsman or hapless man or Slav let the price on his head be forty grivnas.'*

Nevertheless the rules of correct warfare were strict. For example Vladimir, after returning from exile, sent a formal challenge to his rival Yaropolk in Kiev – *'I intend to attack you'* – this being a proper demonstration of honour and courage. When Yaropolk shut himself up in Kiev, Vladimir's *Varjazi* demanded the right to attack and pillage the city *'at the rate of two grivny per man'*. But Vladimir had no wish to see his future capital looted, so he negotiated a surrender instead.

Religion

Before converting to Christianity, Vladimir tried to use a revised version of paganism to strengthen his domination over Rus' territory. This included human sacrifice and what Christian choniclers described as 'debauchery'. Islamic observers were more objective, Ibn Rusta noting that: *'When a boy is born to any man amongst them, he takes a drawn sword to the newborn child and places it between his hands and says to him, I shall bequeath to you no wealth and you will have nothing except what you gain for yourself by this your sword'*. In Vladimir's day Rus' and eastern Slav paganism was a sophisticated religion with large temples, decorated idols, perhaps an organized priesthood and oracles. Perun, as god of war, was favoured by the warriors of the *Druzhina* who, if they wanted to confirm an oath, laid their weapon before an idol of Perun while declaring that those who broke their oaths would become *'yellow as gold and be destroyed by their own weapons'*. With the coming of Christianity monster-slaying saints became particularly popular in Russia, St. George being identified with the pagan

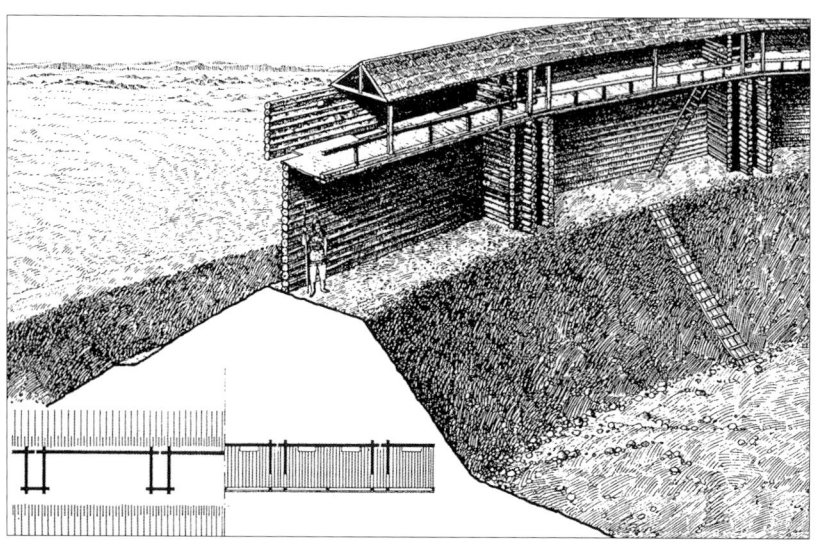

Reconstruction, ground and first-floor plans of the wall of a large 11th-12th century fortified town. (APN)

god Svarog and also being seen as 'master of the wolves'. Perun with his axe or hammer was merged with St.Elias, who crossed the sky in a fiery chariot, and with Russian folk heroes like Il'ya Muromets.

Vladimir's streamlined pagan pantheon failed to provide the necessary political rewards, so he sought a new religion. The Judaism of the previous Khazars was considered, along with Islam and Christianity. In the end Vladimir made a political choice. The Byzantine Empire was close without being threatening. It was an important trade partner and had much to teach the Rus'. There were already many Christians in Vladimir's realm, even in some *Druzhinas*. Consequently he placed the Rus' under Byzantine Orthodox tutelage rather than that of Catholic Western Europe. Nevertheless, the Rus' continued to cultivate their robust image, leading a simple life, washing infrequently, and eating roasted rather than boiled meat. Meanwhile the slave trade continued, many of its victims being Christians captured in various Rus' raids.

Vladimir's decision to accept Orthodox Christianity had enormous implications by changing the ruler of Rus' from a Turkish-style *Khagan* to a European prince, and ultimately a Byzantine *Tsar* or Caesar. The implications of choosing Orthodox rather than Latin-Catholic Christianity were not apparent for several centuries, but they would eventually separate Russia almost as markedly from Western Europe as it was from the Turco-Mongol and Islamic worlds.

THE GOLDEN AGE OF KIEV

The reorientation of Kievan identity made necessary a massive mobilization to strengthen the vulnerable south. New forts were also built and garrisoned by reluctant northern tribes; Kiev had to retain control of the north, which served as a launching pad for Viking raids in the Baltic. Civil wars also tore Rus' apart after Vladimir's death in 1015, and the true golden age of Kiev only began with the accession of Yaroslav as *Veliki Knjazi* – 'Grand Prince' – in 1036.

The Golden Gate of Kiev, originally built in 1037 but reconstructed in 1982.

Many craftsmen, probably including armourers, moved to Kiev after the fall of the Khazars and the population became extremely cosmopolitan, with immigrants arriving from the Islamic world and Scandinavia as well as Slavs and Finns from the rest of Russia. In military terms Kievan Rus' became a melting pot of eastern and western traditions, tactics, arms and armour. The military and political elite was itself of mixed origins, including families of Slav, Scandinavian, Alan, Ossetian, Circassian, eastern Magyar, Turkish and other origins, though all now spoke a Slavic language. Most townsmen were legally free, though there were also slaves, and the tiny middle class provided urban militias whose military importance grew rapidly. Meanwhile the status of women, even those from the *boyar* aristocracy, remained low.

The new titles of *Knjazi* ('Prince') and *Veliki Knjazi* ('Grand' or 'Most Brilliant Prince') gradually replaced the old title of *Khagan* in the 12th century. Succession to the throne of Grand Prince was theoretically based upon a system of rotation amongst those eligible, but in reality might remained more important than right. This led to almost continuous civil wars, until a conference of Rus' princes in 1097 regularized the system – though even this did not stop competion

between rivals, each supported by their own *Druzhina*. The result was a sort of federation which was more stable and effective than is generally recognized. Towns continued to grow, ruled either by a member of the Rurikid princely family or by a *posadnik* governor appointed by one such prince and supported by an armed retinue. Another interesting aspect of Kievan administration, particularly in the north, was the use of birchbark rather than parchment as a writing material. The traditional *Russkaya Pravda* legal code was also updated – even specifying, for example, the compensation required if a person was struck with the blunt hilt of a sword or with a metal goblet. Clearly legal fines were an important source of revenue with which to pay the *Druzhina* and purchase military equipment.

A *Druzhina* remained a prince's immediate source of military power; but during the 11th century urban militias took over from tribal levies as the second most important. Tribal levies generally declined to the status of ill-equipped rural auxiliaries, and more important third sources of troops were nomadic peoples from the neighbouring steppes. It was these varied forces which enabled Kievan Rus' to steadily expand. Most success was achieved in the north and east, since Vladimir's attempt to thrust westwards had failed. To the south the powerful Pechenegs and subsequently the Kipchaks barred expansion; and even in the east the Volga Bulgars remained technologically more advanced that the Rus'.

TOP **Detail from Russian or Byzantine inlaid bronze bowl, late 12th-13th C, showing a rider with a couched spear. (Hermitage Museum, St.Petersburg)**

ABOVE **Detail from a gilded silver bowl, southern Russian or Byzantine, 11th-12th C. Cavalrymen with both spear and bow are shown, wearing long garments depicted in a pattern of diamond-shaped chequers with central dots. (Hermitage Museum, St.Petersburg)**

In Novgorod the ruling princes were little more than commanders of the local army, with other powers being shared by the bishop and the *Veche* town council. Not that this arrangement made Novgorod less warlike: the expansion of the principality (later republic) of Novgorod was more dramatic than that of any other Rus' state. In the vast, inhospitable expances of the taiga and tundra the indigenous Finns and Ugrians were too few to offer much resistance. Meanwhile *ushkúynik* river pirates and Rus' merchants both lived at the expense of local tribes, who were forced to provide furs, fish and hugely valuable walrus ivory. By the mid-12th century Novgorod had established a network of *pogost* administrative centres as far as the White Sea and the Pinega river, where tribute was collected and garrisons kept the trade routes open. More experienced Novgorodian merchants even ventured beyond the Ural mountains to trade with Ugrians and even Samoyeds of the Ob basin.

In the south the Rus' controlled the Azov region and Tmutarakan, strengthening their contact with Byzantium and the Christian states in the Caucasus. The prince of Tmutarakan also seems to have tried to take over former Khazar lands towards the Caspian Sea. This optimistic scenario collapsed, however, with the arrival of the Seljuk Turks and a revival of Islamic power, while Tmutarakan fell to Byzantine control by 1118.

In the fertile south-west Kiev was in competion with several neighbours including Byzantium. Here, in what eventually became western Ukraine and Moldavia-Moldova, Rus' ambitions clashed with Poles, Hungarians and steppe nomads. The situation was equally tense in the south-east, where the Rus' principality of Pereyaslavl was particularly exposed to steppe raiders. In the north-east the Rostov-Suzdal area fell under Rus' control in the 10th century, but did not have its own princes until new towns were established at Suzdal and Vladimir. In fact Suzdalia, as it came to be known, remained a wild frontier region, rich in furs and opportunities, where Rus' tribute-gathering expeditions competed with the Volga Bulgars for domination over neighbouring pagan tribes.

The 12th century saw *Veche* town councils and militias become increasingly important. Meanwhile the leaders of the wealthy merchant class often allied with the local prince's *Druzhina* to dominate the *Veche* council. The *Druzhinas* of those princes who ruled wealthy principalities grew into large, well-equipped forces rivalling those of the Grand Prince himself. Yet these provincial *Druzhinas* were rarely strong enough to face an external aggressor on their own. In such circumstances princes tended to join forces, usually under the leadership of the Grand Prince.

Though the Pechenegs resisted Rus' attempts to dominate the western steppes they were pushed further south, doubling the width of a 'neutral zone' from onc to two days' march. The Kipchaks re-established nomad control of the western steppes by 1120, and created a vast new empire whose two 'wings' were divided by the Ural river. Only the western 'wing' concerned the Rus', and a relatively stable frontier was eventually established. Some Kipchaks converted to Islam, others to Christianity or Judaism in the mid-12th century. The latter played an important role in the 13th century Rus' pricipality of Galich, and their descendants still exist as the Karaims. Although the Kipchaks were formidable neighbours, they were also potent allies with whom several Rus' ruling families intermarried.

Rus' relations with neighbours to the west largely settled down by the later 11th century, while relations with the Byzantine Empire could be described as those between a brash,

Model of the medieval city of Vladimir. (Historical Museum, Vladimir)

expansionist and increasingly powerful student and an ancient, cultured but militarily declining teacher. In fact the Rus' might have taken over the rump of Byzantine territory in the Balkans following the catastrophic Seljuk conquest of Byzantium's Anatolian provinces, had the Crusades not bolstered a Byzantine revival.

THE ARMIES OF KIEVAN RUS'

Among the most distinctive troops in Rus' were the **Varjazi** or, as they were known in Greek, *Varangians*. As in the Byzantine Empire, these formed a distinct group of Scandinavian mercenaries who served only the richest princes. Many arrived in Russia as ready-made armies led by exiled members of the Scandinavian aristocracy, often with their own ships as well as weaponry. Some early *Varjazi* bands were like military brotherhoods with their own pagan religious heirarchy. *Varjazi* leaders were sometimes given the role of *voevodo* or army commander, even in the Christian 11th century; one of the best known was Harald Hardrada, who eventually became King of Norway and died while invading England in 1066. His extraordinary career was recorded in *King Harald's Saga*. This quoted one of Harald's court poets, Thjodolf, on how Harald fought alongside Earl Rognvald in the service of Prince Yaroslav when Harald and Rognval's son were supposedly made commanders of the *Druzhina*: '*Side by side the two leaders fought. Shoulder to shoulder their men lined up. They drove the Slavs into defeat and gave the Poles scant mercy.*' In fact Harald stayed in Russia for several years before going to Byzantium, where he had even stranger adventures. However, the flow of Scandinavian warriors largely dried up by the early 12th century, while the descendants of those who settled in Russia were assimilated.

Less exotic but far more important were the **Druzhina** standing armies which followed each Rus' prince. The name *Druzhina* originally meant a 'community', whose *Drug* 'comrades' were bound together by *Zadruzni* 'communal' bonds. During the late 11th or early 12th century *Malaia* ('small') *Druzhinas* appeared. These consisted of between 25 and several hundred close companions and advisors – sufficient for personal protection and law enforcement, but not for large military campaigns. The closest and most trusted bodyguard of *Otroki* 'youths' were drawn from the *Malaia Druzhina*, while the *Grid'* or 'junior' *Druzhina* consisted of ordinary retainers, servants, assistants and soldiers.

The Golden Gate of Vladimir today; it was originally built in 1164 without the circular corner butresses. (Author's photograph)

The only figure on the mid-12th century bronze doors of Novgorod Cathedral that was made in Russia. It portrays Master Abraham, who assembled the other bronze panels from Germany. (*In situ* Cathedral of Santa Sofia, Novgorod; author's photograph)

The distinction between *Grid'* and *Malaia Druzhina* increased by the late 12th century. So did the cost of maintaining a *Druzhina*. Like their Western and Islamic counterparts, the Rus' princes were constantly attempting to maximize their revenues. Meanwhile the men of a *Druzhina* were bound by oaths to their prince and to each other, these chains of loyalty having more in common with the *istina* 'patronage' seen in early medieval Islamic armies than with the homage system of Western Europe. In return the *Druzhinas* formed highly mobile mounted forces capable of covering huge distances and with few local ties to stop them following their prince wherever he went. As such they again had more in common with their Islamic counterparts than with Western European knights. The status of a *Druzhina* is described in the *Adventures of Prince Igor*, a late 12th century epic which survives in a later form: 'And my men of Kursk are glorious warriors, swaddled under trumpets, cradled under helmets, nursed at the spear's point. To them the roads are known and the valleys are familiar, bent are their bows, open their quivers, sharpened their swords.'

Not all landed aristocrats served in a *Druzhina*, while not all members of a *Druzhina* were of noble origin. Furthermore a member of a *Druzhina* did not lose his lands if he decided to withdraw from the force. Some of the *Druzhina* came from humble backgrounds, climbing to prominence through skill, loyalty and luck. Others came from families which had served a particular princely clan for generations, either in his *Druzhina* or as *posadnik* town governors. Most had been Slav-speaking since the 11th century, though men of different ethnic origins – including Scandinavians, Turks, Kosogian-Circassians and Ossetians from the Caucasus – were probably also found among the *Izgoi* 'hired men' in several *Druzhinas*.

Princes naturally turned to their *Malaia Druzhina* for senior administrative and military personnel such as the *ognishchanin* 'bailiff', *koniushi* 'master of horse', *tiun* 'steward', *podiezdnoi* 'adjutant' and *voevodo* 'army commander'. Similarly the princes used their *Druzhinas* to fight each other, and it was common for a *Druzhina* to remain with their prince through years of ill-fortune, privation and even exile.

In purely military terms a *Druzhina* formed a small but well-equipped and highly trained fighting force. Travel rather than fighting dominated their lives, as one prince might rule several different principalities during his life. In addition his men gathered tribute, and confronted troublesome cousins. The *Druzhinas* adopted cavalry warfare as a result of experience fighting steppe nomads in the south. Their love of hunting, sometimes on a vast scale over several days, may again have reflected steppe influence. For any prince keeping his *Druzhina* intact was a primary consideration – other troops could be squandered, but not the *Druzhina*, who were, in any case, too few to have a decisive impact. Nor were *Druzhinas* equipped for siege warfare; in such circumstances they could do little without the support of urban militias.

The second most important source of troops were, in fact, these **militias.** The earliest were drawn from Slav and other tribes. In late 10th century Chernigov, for example, a local militia seem to have defended the area while the Rus' warrior elite were raiding elsewhere. But from the 11th century onwards urban militias became more significant. Since the tribal era militias had theoretically been divided into *tysiacha* 'thousands', although such numbers reflected the traditional Turco-Mongol system of dividing steppe armies on a decimal basis rather than the reality of Rus' military units. Each was supposedly led by a *tysiatsky* 'commander of a thousand'; and in later years the roles of *tysiatsky* and *voevodo* merged.

The Slav, Finn and Scandinavian merchant class which dominated Russian *Veche* town councils may have been the same men who filled the ranks of the militia, but it is less clear whether more temporary inhabitants took part. There were, for example, Armenian colonies in several places, and in 1064 a group of Armenian soldiers reportedly took part in a campaign against Poland. Given the advanced technology and military reputation of Armenians around this time, their presence is likely to have been welcomed. Occasionally a militia was incorporated into a *Druzhina*, though this was probably a temporary expedient. The loyalty of militias was, however, to their own towns, and a prince could not take them for granted, particularly if a campaign was directed against other Rus' rather than a foreign invader.

In Novgorod and probably in other towns the militia was based upon almost autonomous quarters, each of which was responsible for the defensive wall in its part of town. By the early 13th century some larger militias had evolved simple systems of organization. Officer ranks now included the *sotski* or *sotnik* commanding one of the *sotnia* 'hundreds', as well as the *tysiatsky*. The latter was selected by the *Veche* town council while serving as a sort of police chief.

Domes of the 12th century Cathedral of Santa Sofia above the 15th century fortifications of Novgorod's Kremlin. (Author's photograph)

The local prince normally provided the militias were arms, armour and horses. Perhaps as a result their weaponry was simple, though wealthier cities probably armed their own militias by the 13th century. According to the German *Livonian Rhymed Chronicle* the Pskov militia included crossbowmen as well as archers, while many also wore shining 'cuirasses'. Several towns owed their prosperity to their control of portage routes between major rivers which needed defending, while others provided guides who might help a prince's *Druzhina* to find their elusive nomad foe.

In the 11th century the **Voi** or tribal levies fought on foot with spears and axes. Though the importance of tribal *Voi* slumped by the 12th century, rural recruitment from the villages remained necessary for lesser princes who controlled only one town. Those mustered in such a manner were known as *Smerd*, which meant peasants, and they only appeared during emergencies. In the late 12th and early 13th centuries an armed peasantry virtually disappeared, and those peasants who did have a military role fulfilled it by providing food and transport.

Black Hoods, Allies and Others

Although some Slav tribes had traditions of horsemanship and the Scandinavian Rus' soon learned to fight on horseback, the problem of a lack of cavalry remained. Consequently the Rus' enlisted horsemen from nomadic steppe peoples. Amongst the first such allies were Torks who accompanied a Rus' army in the late 10th century, while Pechenegs provided cavalry and horse-archers in the 11th century. The Grand Prince of Kiev sought mounted mercenaries elsewhere; Poles, Germans and Hungarians are all mentioned. Men of steppe origin were far more important, however, and after the Kipchaks ousted the Pechenegs they in turn appeared as Rus' auxiliaries (though Russian chroniclers often accused them of being interested in plunder rather than fighting). Prince Mstislav of Tmutarakan also recruited many warriors 'from beyond the steppes', which suggests the settled rather than nomadic peoples of the Caucasus mountains; while mid-13th century Novgorod recruited amongst the local Finn tribes of the Gulf of Finland.

Wall painting of St.George, c.1167. (*In situ* Church of St.George, Starya Ladoga)

The so-called *Chernye Klobuki* or 'Black Hoods' were different. When one steppe tribe was defeated by another, the defeated military elite traditionally moved on or accepted subordinate status under the new rulers. When such people reached the western end of the steppes they effectively had nowhere else to go, as the rise of powerful European states removed the option of taking over the Hungarian Plain or conquering territory in the Balkans. Consequently, following the arrival of the Kipchaks, part of the defeated Pechenegs, Torks and Berends sought refuge in the wooded-steppe borderlands of southern Russia, where they were generally welcomed by Rus' princes.

During the late 11th century these military immigrants evolved into the *Chernye Klobuki* or, in Turkish, the *Karakalpak*. Both names meant Black Hoods or Hats, after the characteristic headgear of these nomads. For their part the eclectic nature of nomad culture made it relatively easy for them to fit into their new environment, where they – like those who settled within Hungarian territory – defended their patrons' frontiers against each other and against new invaders.

Stone icon of St.Demetrius made in south-western Russia, early 13th century. (Historical Museum, Kamenez-Podolsk)

For a while the Torks, who were related to the Oghuz who conquered most of the eastern Islamic world in the 11th century, formed the main element of the *Chernye Klobuki*. They settled in the Ros river basin, along the forest frontier, the Bukovina and the northern slopes of the Carpathian mountains, forming autonomous warrior communities around small *gorod* wood and timber forts. The Berends arrived under similar circumstances around the same time.

The social and military organization of the *Chernye Klobuki* was different to that of the Rus'. For example, the Torks' leader was recognized as a prince by the Rus' and the *Chernye Klobuki* retained much of their tribal structure. Archaeological and documentary evidence also shows that they were numerous, well-armed and prosperous; their leaders often wore silk headgear, silver chains and earrings made in Russia, while most had converted to Christianity by the late 12th century. By then *Chernye Klobuki* of Berend and perhaps other origins were formed into regular military forces. They proved effective against Poles and Hungarians, defended the west bank of the Dnieper from 'civilized' Kipchaks, but were particularly hostile to the *Dikie Polovsty* or 'wild Kipchaks' east of that river. After the Kipchaks took control of the

Labourer resting – a 13th C manuscript illustration – rotated here for clarity – from Pskov. (MS no.3, State Historical Museum, Moscow)

Prince kneeling before an archangel; 13th century gold-inlaid bronze doors. (*In situ* Rozhdestvensky Monastery, Suzdal; author's photograph)

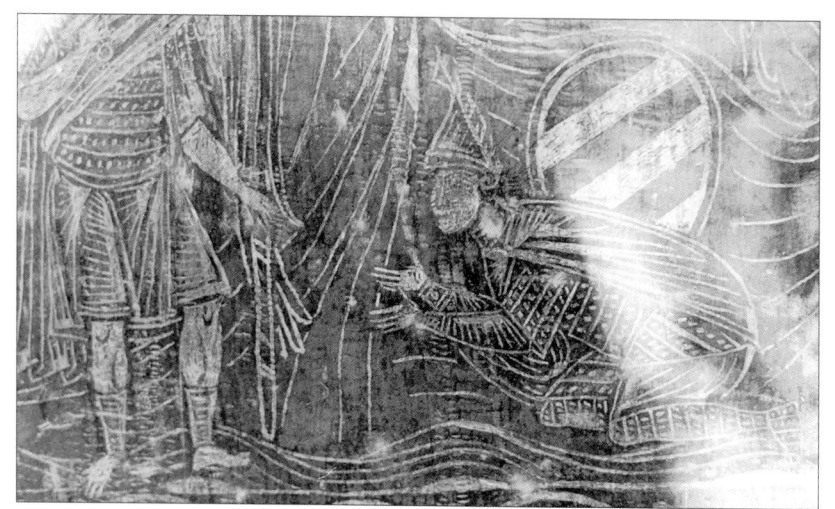

western steppes in the late 11th century they too became a source of allies and mercenaries, though not yet of *Chernye Klobuki*. Shortly before 1230 AD most of those living in what are now Moldova and Moldavia converted to Catholic Christianity, and it seemed as if the Kipchaks would be absorbed into the mainsteam of European civilization. But a new threat was already on the horizon – the Mongols, who would sweep the Kipchak elite into oblivion while absorbing the rest.

Among various other settled and semi-nomadic peoples were the *Brodniki*, who were fisherfolk living along the banks of the southern Don and other rivers within Rus' and Kipchak territory. They had much in common with the later Cossacks in military terms, particularly in their reluctance to accept outside control, and in their use of rivers as sources of food and refuges from attack.

Morale and Motivation

Ransom from prisoners and the capture of slaves was a major source of income for the Rus' military elite in the 10th and early 11th centuries, booty and ransom remaining the reason for conducting many campaigns thoughout the 12th century. Meanwhile military attitudes often had more in common with those of the Byzantine Empire and Islamic world than with Western Europe or the Turco-Mongols. Fatal violence was minimized and full-scale battles were avoided whenever possible. Fear of shame was seemingly stronger than desire for glory, and concepts of individual honour were less highly developed than amongst the European knightly class. In fact honour tended to be associated with the group, primarily the *Druzhina*, or to be focussed upon service to a prince. Even loyalty was viewed differently, and members of a *Druzhina* could withdraw whenever they wished without disgrace. Only if a warrior offered his service to a foreign or a non-Orthodox Christian ruler would he be regarded as a traitor.

Military status had been displayed through the carrying of decorated weaponry in the 10th century, though this fashion declined in subsequent years. The remarkable *Epic of Prince Igor* includes other insights into late 12th and early 13th century Rus' military attitudes, as when it declares: *'The sons of Rus' have crossed the great plains with their scarlet shields, seeking honour for themselves and glory for the prince'*. And, *'No longer do I see at the helm* (of the boat) *my brother Yaroslav, strong, rich and mighty in warriors, with his Chernigov boyars, his valient Druzhina, with the Tatrans and Shelbirs and Topchaks and Revugs and Olbers* (subordinate tribes), *without shields, only knife-blade in boot. With war-whoops they vanquish hosts, sounding the glory of their grandsires'*.

Religion played an increasingly important part

in military motivation, with attachment to the Orthodox Church becoming the primary expression of Russian self-identity. From the late 12th century onwards differences between the Catholic and Orthodox Churches became more pronounced, particularly after the Fourth Crusade captured the Byzantine capital of Constantinople and began persecuting those who followed the Orthodox rite.

Yet Orthodox Christianity was no more peaceable than Catholic, and although it did not develop a Crusading mentality, military saints featured prominently in Orthodox hagiography, particularly amongst the Rus'. It was rare for early Christian Rus' rulers to pray to God for victory, and this only became normal in the 12th and 13th centuries. By then chroniclers habitually ascribed success in battle to divine favour, with defeat being blamed on the sinfulness of the defeated ruler – particularly when defeated by non-Christians, who were seen as instruments of God's wrath. There was, however, a distinction between death in battle with non-Christians and true martyrdom. For the Orthodox, martyrdom was a willing acceptance of death without any attempt at self-defence. Kissing crosses or icons soon played a major part in oath-taking ceremonies, but belief in miracle-working icons which influenced the outcome of battles was not seen until the 14th century.

Members of the Church took an active part in political and military matters. For instance, the 12th century monk Daniel had been a soldier, and it was for this reason that he was sent as a diplomatic messenger to the Crusader Kingdom of Jerusalem. He was to see whether Kiev could act to ease the passage of Scandinavian recruits for the armies of the Crusader States. On the other hand, many pagan beliefs persisted amongst Rus' warriors. The sacrificing of favourite horses during funerary ceremonies continued despite superficial conversion to Christianity. The *Druzhinas* tended to belief in oracles or omens. Another pagan survival was the *postrig* ceremony, when a four- or five-year-old boy's hair was cut for the first time. Even in the 13th century this marked his move from childhood to noble status, civic responsibilities and his first ride on horseback.

The adoption of Christianity also had a profound impact on Rus' military symbolism. During the 10th century pagan Rus' *Khagans* are said to have adopted Turkish-style tribal *tamgas* as marks of authority. Thereafter the Rus' ruling elite and perhaps their military followers adopted the Byzantine habit of painting 'name saints' on their shields. The *Epic of Prince Igor* also refers to scarlet shields and a white flag on a scarlet staff, as well as a scarlet horse-tail banner in a silver socket – the latter obviously copied from steppe peoples. Very little is known about

Detail – Prince Yaroslav Vsevolodovich offering his church to Christ; wall painting, c.1246. (*In situ* Church of the Saviour, Nereditsa)

Aerial view of the Kremlin of Novgorod, taken before the Second World War.

military music in medieval Rus', though the German *Livonian Rhymed Chronicle* stated that the Rus' used drums and fifes or trumpets to re-assemble their men after a retreat or a river crossing.

COSTUME, ARMS & ARMOUR

Scandinavian styles lasted for a time in clothing and decoration of weapons, but other influences were soon apparent. A Byzantine description of the *Khagan* Sviatoslav after his capture in 971 AD stated that he wore a plain white tunic the same as his followers' but cleaner, and a gold ring in one ear, while his head was shaved except for one long lock which was thought to indicate nobility. This Asiatic hairstyle was seen amongst Hungarians, Bulgarians, some steppe tribes and of course the later Cossacks. According to another Byzantine writer the *Varjazi/Varangians* did not shave, pluck their eyebrows or use make-up like the Italo-Normans and Byzantines. The Arab traveller Ibn Fadlan described the Rus' who traded with the Volga Bulgars as wearing quilted jerkins and large cloaks thrown over one shoulder so that their sword-arm remained free.

By the 12th century a more Oriental Russian costume had evolved. It was much the same for all classes except that the wealthy wore imported silk brocades. In summer men wore a linen shirt and trousers which were used as underclothes in winter, plus a kaftan-like *svita*, a *koch* overcoat and a *miatelia* mantle or cloak which was popular in western Russia. The *korzno* was the elaborate mantle of the ruling class. Sheepskin and the fur of bear, wolf or marten was worn in winter; the *kozhukh* was close-waisted and long-sleeved, whereas the *shuba* was looser. Fur hats were worn by all classes. *Sapogi* high boots and *cherevi* shoes could be made of fine leather, and many found by archaeologists at Novgorod had decorative patterns. In contrast the poor had footwear made of *bast* birch bark.

Court clothing was strongly influenced by Byzantium, while fine fabrics were imported from Constantinople, the Islamic world or Western Europe. The *Galich Chronicle* indicated that the *boyar* aristocracy of south-western Russia looked similar to the knightly class of neighbouring Poland, while Friar William of Rubruck described the men of mid-13th century Ruthenia-Galich as wearing *'capes like the Germans, and on their heads they wear felt caps, pointed and very high.'*

Russia was relatively rich in iron and the Poljane tribe of the Kiev region had capable armourers in the 9th century. Nevertheless, most Western historians have emphasized external technological influences rather than looking at local Slav traditions, while Soviet historians tended to denigrate Turco-Mongol influence in

Late 12th-early 13th C Russian icon of St.Demetrius. What appears to be a scale cuirass is visible at the upper arms and across the lap; the lower legs are wrapped with cloth strips puttee-style. (Tretyakov Gallery, Moscow)

SOUTHERN RUSSIA, 12th C
1: Grand Prince of Kiev
2: Palace guardsman
3 & 4: Noblewoman and child

favour of that from Scandinavia. Consequently a distorted image has emerged.

By the mid-10th century arms, armour and horse-harness were being made in several Rus' cities. By the 12th century the volume and quantity of production was high, although as yet Russian steel remained of a brittle type, suitable for files but not elastic enough for blades. Meanwhile imported equipment remained fashionable among the elite, often decorated locally or modified for the specialized needs of Rus' warriors. Bronze sword hilts and scabbard fittings were made locally, while Novgorod was famous for its workers in leather and wood – the latter ranging from boxwood dagger handles and shields to ship-building.

Migrating warriors habitually took their own weaponry with them, and similarly, some brought equipment home again. For example, Harald Sigurdson kept a Byzantine armour which he nicknamed 'Emma', while another Icelandic Varangian returned in about 1030 with gilded arms, armour, horse-harness, and a shield on which a supposed 'knight' was painted – almost certainly a warrior saint. The *Chernye Klobuki* similarly entered Rus' service with their own arms, armour and harness, which were described as superior to those of the Rus' themselves. Within Rus' it was also normal for princes to reward faithful followers by giving them arms, armour and high quality clothing, just as was done in the Islamic world.

Helmet of Prince Yaroslav Vsevolodovich, c.1206-67. (Kremlin Museum, Moscow).

Though weapony changed over the years, it did not follow the same path as in Western Europe. In the 8th and 9th centuries the Slavs used shields, spears, javelins, axes and bows, but by the 10th century they were armed in virtually the same manner as the Scandinavian Rus'. The latter were equipped like typical Vikings with mail hauberks, swords, single-edged axes, large wooden shields with iron bosses, and decorative arm-rings.

By the end of the 10th century a more distinctively Russian armoury had evolved which did not change much over the next two centuries. The best might consist of a silver- or gold-plated iron helmet, mail hauberk, bow and leather quiver, sabre in a silver-mounted scabbard, silvered mace and iron spear. This was essentially a mixture of Eastern and Western styles, whereas horse-harness remained Eastern until the 12th century when Western forms were adopted by the *Druzhinas*. Nevertheless steppe influence remained more important than any other. Even the *Druzhinas'* use of heavy lances, substantial body armour and close combat shock tactics was as likely to stem from the armoured cavalry elites of the steppes as from Western Europe or Byzantium. In this respect the Khazars and Magyars were the most significant influences during the formative years of Rus'. Rus' adoption of horse-archery was an even clearer example of military influence from the steppes; while the speed with which some *Druzhinas* adopted Mongol arms and armour in the 13th century suggests that differences were not that great.

Nevertheless, Rus' military equipment remained a hybrid style designed to cope with static European armies in the north and mobile steppe forces in the south. *Druzhina* cavalry used both sword and sabre, couched lance and lighter spear, single-edged Scandinavian *seax* and Eastern mace, while archers used barbed European arrows as well as armour-piercing Eastern arrows. One description of the Prince of Suzdal's *Druzhina* mentions swords, tall or pointed helmets, *barmitsa* mail aventails, apparently cuirasses rather than mail hauberks, perhaps leg defences, and kite-shaped shields. Northern Rus' cavalry were similar, but since the 11th century the infantry who played a major role in this region had been equipped with javelin or spear, small axe, large dagger, bows for younger men and helmets for the wealthy. Mail had been used since the 7th century, while a form of scale or lamellar cuirass appeared in the 11th or 12th centuries, becoming more common in the 13th. Archaeological excavations also unearthed other weaponry at Novgorod, including toy wooden swords and small bows for children. Crossbows were used from the late 12th or early 13th century onwards but as yet this weapon only seems to have been used in north-western Russia.

WARFARE IN A BROAD ARENA

Medieval Russian campaigns were often conducted over huge distances in a country where rivers dominated strategy. They served as waterways in summer, while in the north and east rivers served as smooth pathways for sledges, men and animals in winter. 'Frost nails' for the feet of men and horses had been known since the 9th century, enabling both to walk over smooth ice without slipping; and in the north overland travel was, in fact, easier in winter than other seasons. The worst times for movement were spring and autumn, these being the muddy seasons of *rasputitsa*, 'roadlessness', caused by rain, melting snow or thawing ice. An unseasonal thaw could also send ice floes floating down-river to smash wooden bridges. In the south Rus' armies used large waggons when campaigning over long distances, but since these easily bogged down in mud boats were preferred.

The size of rivers was not important so long as they could take relatively shallow-draft boats. River fleets normally beached for the night, and although settlements along the rivers provided food and rest a network of such stopping places was not completed before the 13th century. Nevertheless several inland bases were established during the 10th century, the most remarkable being a large fortified harbour at Voyn near the confluence of the Sula and Dnieper, with another 'naval base' two kilometres upstream. These were assembly points for convoys sailing across the steppe, and they probably had cavalry garrisons, perhaps of *Chernye Klobuki*, who would ride along the banks beside the boats to ward off nomad attack. On the Dnieper river estuary Olesh'e was developed late in the 10th century as a safe base from which convoys could sail around the Black Sea coast.

Similar dangers faced river travellers in other frontier regions, both from Finno-Ugrian tribes and *ushkúynik* river pirates. Portages, where ships had to be hauled overland from one river to another or around rapids, remained places of danger, though the most important were

Gilded helmet with mail aventail, from a chieftain's grave at Cingul Kurgan. (Museum of Historical Treasures, Kiev)

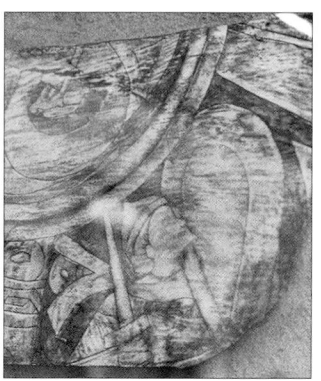

Part of a 12th C carved wooden disc from Novgorod showing a warrior with a sword and kite-shaped shield. (Kremlin Museum, Novgorod)

sometimes garrisoned by local troops. Some were even paved with timber, while canals were dug around the most serious obstacles. Portages were, of course, strategically as well as economically significant; for example, the Dnieper rapids remained a major military headache throughout the year. Here boats were normally unloaded and lightened so that they could be poled or pulled through before being reloaded on the other side of the rapids.

Sea communication was of secondary importance and medieval Rus' never established a secure outlet to the Baltic, while the White Sea led only to the frozen Arctic. The Black Sea was notoriously stormy and was dominated first by the Byzantines and subsequently by the Italians. Little is in fact known about Rus' ships, and it is unclear whether they had much in common with Viking vessels. Where rivercraft were concerned the Rus' had many traditions to draw upon. The Slavs, Finno-Ugrians and Turks had rafts, inflated skins, dug-out canoes, large hide-covered coracles and boats of sewn plant matter, while the Rus' mostly used flat-bottomed boats and rafts.

Terrain and weather influenced both armies and tactics. In general infantry dominated Rus' warfare up to the 10th century, and cavalry from the 11th century onwards. During the 12th century the horsemen were themselves divided into two types: horse-archers and close combat lance-armed troopers. The majority of horse-archers were probably *Chernye Klobuki* and auxiliaries of steppe origin, while most close-combat horsemen were from the *Druzhinas* which fought in disciplined units like Byzantines or Western European knights.

Foreigners often commented on the number of Rus' archers, but this can be misleading. Infantry archers using longbows had played a significant role in Viking warfare and Rus' infantry skirmishers were also typically armed with bows. In fact written sources from the neighbouring Baltic Crusader states show that Russian archers were feared by both

(A) Helmet from Oskol, probably imported from Iran 8th-9th C (Hermitage Museum, St. Petersburg)
(B) From Novorosiysk, probably from steppes or Byzantium, 850-900 AD (Historical Museum, Novorosiysk)
(C) Varangian style, from western Russia or eastern Poland, 12th-13th C (Army Museum, Warsaw)
(D & E) From Gnezdovo, 10th C (State Historical Museum, Moscow)
(F) From Chernigov, mid-10th C (State Historical Museum, Moscow)
(G) From south-western Russia, possibly Byzantine 12th-13th C (Historical Museum, Kiev)
(H) From Nikolskoye, c.1200 AD (Hermitage Museum, St.Petersburg)
(I) From Babiche, steppe origin 1150-1250 AD (Hermitage Museum, St.Petersburg)
(J) Chernye Klobuki with visor rusted to the front, from Lipovitz, 12th-13th C
(K-M) From Ukraine, 12th-13th C (Hermitage Museum, St.Petersburg).

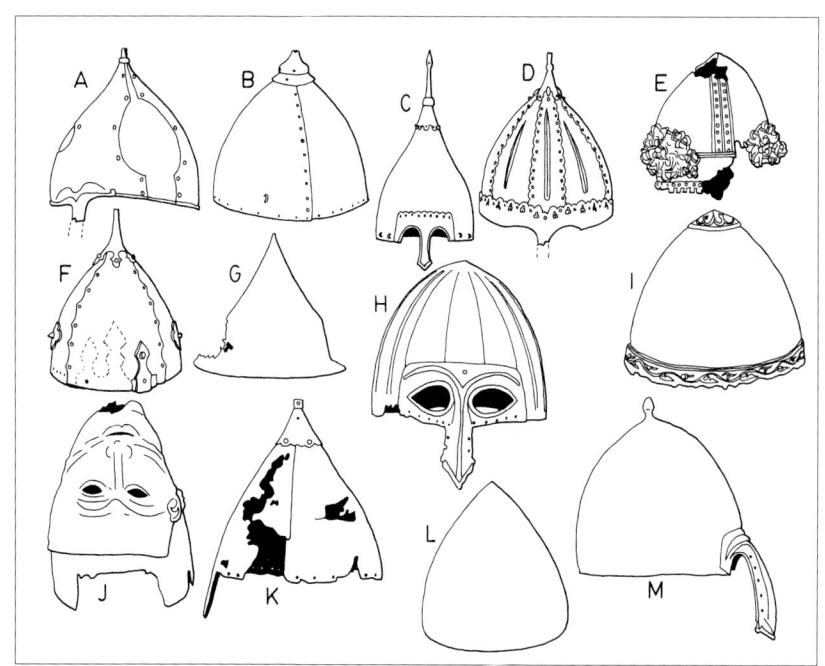

Balts and Crusaders. Elite *Druzhina* cavalry were equipped with bows but they probably used the same static 'shower shooting' tactics as did horse-archers in other non-nomadic armies, notably those of Byzantium and several Islamic states.

Long distances had a major impact on medieval Rus' strategy, great attention being paid to route selection and the obstacles an army might face. The early *Book of Annals* included specific geographical information. Seasonal factors not only effected roads and rivers but also an enemy's strength. The horses of steppe tribes were considered 'ready for war' in autumn, whereas the nomads were most vulnerable in late summer when steppe pasture had been dried up by the sun. Winter warfare was commonplace, though it probably consisted of raiding, sometimes by small groups using skis rather than large armies. The Rus' did, however, campaign in late winter when frosts kept the earth hard after much of the snow had melted.

Rus' princes preferred to attack nomad foes along the river routes, with infantry travelling in boats while cavalry rode along the bank. On the other hand choke-points such as fords or portages could be the scene of ambushes. The use of islands in rivers, lakes or near coasts as military bases was an extension of the same strategy. Islands similarly provided Rus' armies with security when campaigning outside their own territory, since they controlled most waterways.

River raiding tactics were used by the Prince of Polotsk when attempting unsuccessfully to reassert his hegemony over Lett and Liv tribes in 1206. The army sent by the Prince of Suzdal against the Volga Bulgars in 1220 also went by boat. After disembarkation it drew up by units called *polks* – that from Rostov on the right wing, that of Pereyaslavl on the left, that of the Grand Prince of Suzdal in the centre, while

(A) Sword from Kamenez-Podolsk, 10th-11th C
(B) From Novgorod, 9th-10th C
(C) From Gnezdovo, 9th-10th C
(D) From Bor, 9th-10th C
(E-F) 'Sabre of Charlemagne', Russian or Hungarian 950-1025 AD (Kunsthistorisches Museum, Vienna)
(G) From Foscevataja, c.1000 AD
(H) From Grodno, 11th C
(I) From Ukraine, 12th C
(J) From Kiev, 12th-13th C
(K) From Ukraine, 12th C
(L) From tomb of Lithuanian Prince Daumantas, mid-13th C (Historical Museum, Pskov).

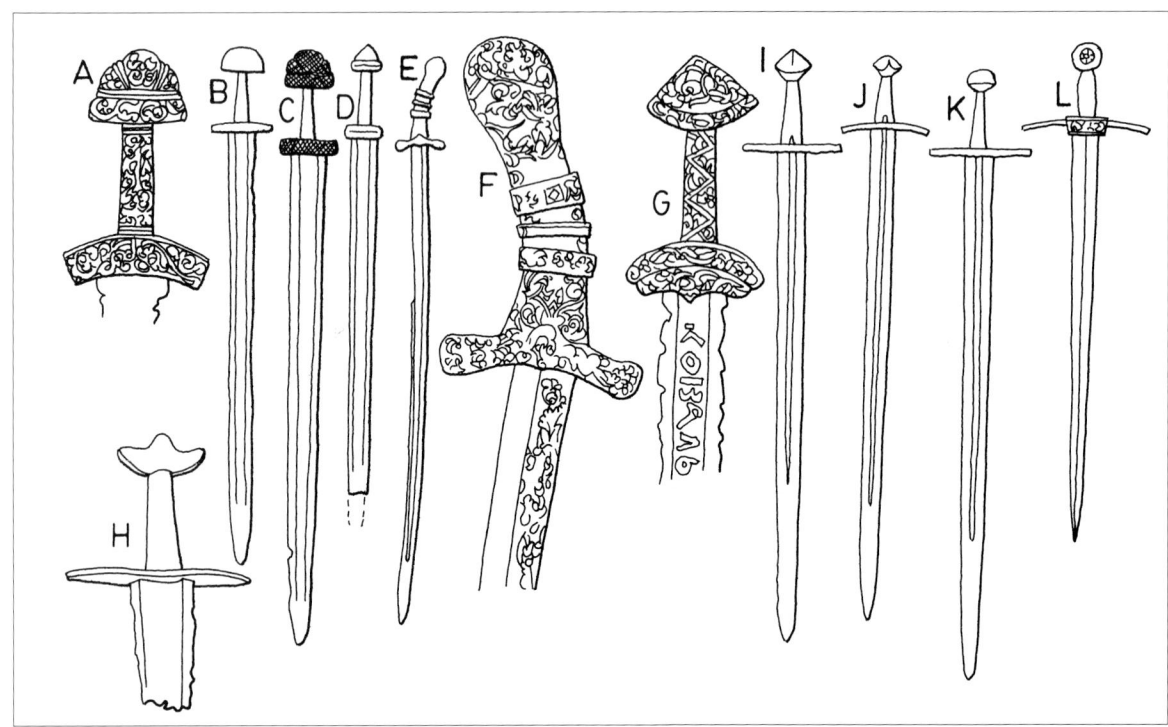

another *polk* guarded the boats. Three years later a much larger army assembled to help the Kipchaks face the Mongols. This time the men of Galich and Volhynia sailed down the Dniester, then along the Black Sea coast to join other Rus' *Druzhinas* on an island in the Dnieper river. A large Rus' force, with its Kipchak allies, then made an amphibious landing under the shot of Mongol archers, and the Grand Prince of Kiev erected a field fortification before joining a nine-day pursuit of the apparently beaten Mongols. Unfortunately the campaign ended in disaster at the battle of the Kalka River. In other steppe regions where rivers were lacking, Rus' forces often clung to scattered woodland or marshes rather than venturing out on to the open grasslands.

Battlefield tactics changed with the adoption of more cavalry. In the early days, for example, a Scandinavian-style *Skjaldbord* or 'shield fort' would be formed around a leader. Rival armies then tried to break the opposition's shield-wall and kill their leader. Subsequent tactical changes reflected both Byzantine and steppe influences, particularly in a Rus' use of waggons as field fortifications.

Nevertheless, greater emphasis seems to have been given to negotiations in serious attempts to resolve quarrels without bloodshed. If this failed a prince would discuss tactics with his *Druzhina* and the leaders of urban militias, none of whom could be ignored. Skirmishing was rare and most battles were fought immediately, with various units entering the fight separately or in sequence.

The importance of the right flank is said to reflect pagan shamanistic beliefs, though in reality it was the same as in all Asian and Middle Eastern armies where the right traditionally took the offensive role. By the 12th century both wings normally consisted of cavalry, with infantry forming the centre which consisted of a shield-wall of *Kopejshchik* spearmen behind which the *Luchnik* or *Strelets* archers could shoot. Meanwhile experience of facing nomad forces taught the Rus' to guard their backs and flanks with obstacles such as forests or rivers. Numerous minor conflicts between rival princes were settled by a show of force, sometimes with a brief clash before the weaker side backed down. As a result serious and prolonged fighting between *Druzhinas* was rare.

The Rus' also fought at night as when, in 1016, Yaroslav faced Sviatopolk. The *Russian Primary Chronicle* described how *'That evening Yaroslav with his troops crossed to the other bank of the Dnieper, and they pushed the boats away from the bank and prepared to make battle that night. Yaroslav said to his Druzhina, put a mark on yourself, wind your heads in kerchiefs. And there was a terrible fight, and before dawn they defeated Sviatopolk.'*

Though most Rus' armies were small, larger forces of 3,000-10,000 men could be mustered for major campaigns. Princes would send envoys to areas under their sometimes nominal control, requesting military support and hiring mercenaries. Allies would be sought, often amongst nomad tribes, and alliances were cemented by public oath-taking. A campaign by the Grand Prince of Suzdalia against the Volga Bulgars in 1220 was probably typical. Here the Grand Prince summoned help from lesser princes who were his brothers, cousins and nephews. Most did not lead their own men to the muster but placed them under the command of *Voevody* army commanders. In fact it was normal for junior princes to obey military commands from senior princes without complaint.

Detail from panel-painted icon of St.Theodore, 1170; note the apparent scale cuirass. (Kremlin Museum, Moscow)

Fortification and Siege Warfare

There was plenty of fortification in Russia before the arrival of the Rus', ranging from the famous 'white stone' forts built by the Khazars to the earth and timber defences erected by Slav colonists further north. But whereas Khazar fortresses were largely symbolic and perhaps served as winter compounds for tribute-collectors, Slav *gorodishche* forts were less impressive but more businesslike. They generally used naturally defensible sites and were designed to resist a single attack by an enemy lacking siege capabilities.

The Scandinavian Rus' arrived with little experience of fortification, but Rus' history saw the development of two distinct forms of timber architecture and fortification. In the far north houses and forts were built with straight coniferous treetrunks. Further south the deciduous timber was rarely straight and as a result wooden walls had to be weatherproofed with plaster and straw. In the deep south semi-sunken houses provided insulation against the searing heat and biting cold of the steppes.

The first Rus' stone fortification may have been a dry limestone circuit wall built at Starya Ladoga around 900 AD. Here slabs were laid directly on the earth with neither foundations nor mortar, though there was at least one tower attached to the inside of the wall. Elsewhere early Rus' fortifications were much the same as those of the previous Slav tribes, being small, relying on a naturally strong position, ditch and rampart. The only exception seems to have been a stone structure within traditional fortifications on one of the hills of Kiev.

Things changed considerably under Vladimir, during whose reign numerous forts were erected along the river routes. Most consisted of wooden walls above earth ramparts reinforced with logs. One example was the citadel of Vasiliev, whose rampart was raised over wooden frames with the outermost section filled with rows of unfired bricks. The walls of the new towns of Belgorod and Pereyaslavl had a core of unfired brick comparable to those in the citadel of Kiev, this system probably having been introduced by Byzantine architects working on the nearby Cathedral of Santa Sofia. The resulting ramparts were presumably topped by a timber wall or palisade. It seems that over a hundred of these fortified towns and settlements were built in southern Russia during the reign of Vladimir. In strategic terms they also had an offensive purpose, serving as bases for expansion.

The most significant change was from the defence of only the most vulnerable side of a naturally strong site to all-round defence, using a mixture of stone, earth, clay and timber. This in turn reflected increasing

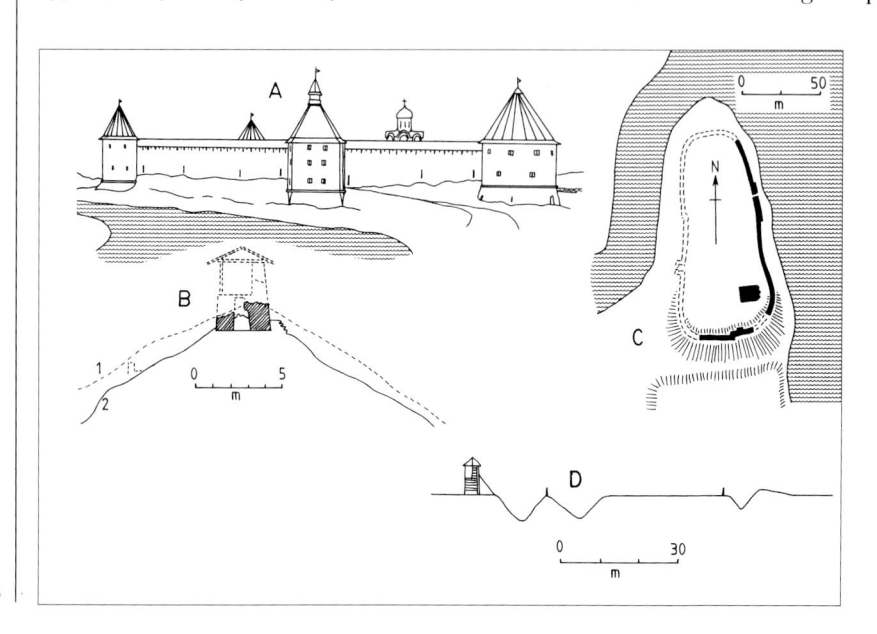

Stone icon of St.George from northern Russia, c.1250. (State Russian Museum, St.Petersburg)

Fortification of Starya Ladoga:
(A) Reconstruction of western wall overlooking Ladozhka river in the 13th century. (Starya Ladoga Historical Museum)
(B) Section through south-eastern wall in 1114 AD: 1 – modern ground level, 2 – original ground level. (after Kirpitchnikov)
(C) Plan view, 12th–13th centuries.
(D) Wall, ditches and advance palisades defending the southern approaches. (after Kirpitchnikov)

Fortress of Kamenez-Podolsk, first built in the 11th C and progressively strengthened until the 16th.

sophistication on the part of those threatening such fortifications. In fact a specifically Russian style of military architecture developed along the steppe frontier rather than in the west of the country. Here some princes received technical help from Byzantine allies. The most ambitious scheme was Grand Prince Yaroslav's new fortifications in and around Kiev, which were intended to include an 'outer shield' of forts and an 'inner shield' of ramparts three and a half kilometres long. Kiev's own earthworks were up to 30 metres wide at the base, 11 metres high, and with a further 5 metres of wooden palisade. Three gates pierced this rampart: the wooden Jew's and Pole's Gates and the stone Golden Gate. This was so-named because above its two-storey-high gateway was a church with a gilded dome (see page 15).

In the west a form of round fortress had developed amongst various Slav tribes, and this style also spread eastwards in the 11th and 12th centuries. Meanwhile in the far south-west, in Galich, the influence of European stone was seen by the later 12th century. A few solitary stone towers appeared in Volhynia but most were only built in the later 13th century. In the bleak north-east the rulers of Suzdal and Rostov built small timber forts to protect their merchants from Novgorod and the Volga Bulgars. In the mid-13th century the increasing threat posed by Lithuanian raiders led to the fortification of the north-western frontier, with Toropets in the principality of Polotsk as a strategic base.

Siege warfare was very rudimentary in the early Rus' era. By the 12th century, however, the *Chernye Klobuki* auxiliaries who garrisoned southern fortresses were skilled in defensive siege warfare, though such capabilities were not evenly spread across the country. In 1206, for example, Rus' helping defend the Lithuanian castle of Holm tried to imitate the German Crusaders' stone-throwing machine, but only succeeded in hurling rocks backwards against their own men. Less than a generation later, when helping defend Tartu, Rus' troops were probably responsible for a 'wheel filled with fire' which the defenders rolled against the Crusaders' siege engines, followed by dry wood thrown from the ramparts. Meanwhile Rus' fortifications themselves reflected a more active form of attack using siege machines and direct assault.

Another remarkable feature of Rus' defences was a series of long walls. Comparable linear walls appeared in Scandinavia, but whether Vikings took the concept to Russia or learned it in the east remains unknown. Enormous linear defences had, of course, been a feature of the Sassanian Empire several centuries earlier. Prince Vladimir was apparently responsible for the so-called 'Snake Ramparts' which are 100 kilometres long. These consisted of successive lines of ramparts south and east of Kiev, as well as ramparts on the left bank of the Dnieper and along the lower course of the Sula river, both associated with the fortified settlement of Voin which incorporated a harbour. Another series of ramparts enclosed Vitichev, a marshalling point for fleets sailing down river to Byzantium.

Russia Divided
By the start of the 13th century Kievan Rus' was a diverse territory with many centres of power dominated by one ruling Rurikid dynasty. In the cultured and peaceable south a stable frontier had been established with the Kipchak Turks. Towns were expanding, as was agriculture, along with a sense of Russian identity based upon a Slav language and the Orthodox Church. The frontiers between principalities meant little, particularly to the princes and their *Druzhinas*, and collapse in the face of the Mongol invasion was not a result of fragmentation. The prestige of Kiev as the centre of Rus' power had, however, declined. Indeed the city had been sacked in 1169, not by foreign foes but by rival Rus' princes.

By the start of the 13th century Russia's centre of gravity had shifted elsewhere. Galich in the south-west was increasingly powerful, and was the only part of medieval Rus' which was to some extent feudalized in a Western European manner. The armies of Volhynia-Galich also resembled those of Poland and Hungary despite still being based upon the traditional *Druzhina*, urban militias and *Chernye Klobuki*. Rus' relations with the Kipchaks were generally friendly, even though the latter were converting to Catholic rather than Orthodox Christianity. Russian relations with what remained of the Byzantine Empire also remained close.

Militarily and politically, however, Suzdalia was now the most powerful part of Rus'. Even the title of *Veliki Knjazi*, Grand Prince, was usually held by the ruler of Suzdalia. This eastern region had been called 'beyond the forest' and it remained a frontier zone. More importantly for the future, the power of the Princes of Suzdalia was not constrained by a strong *boyar* aristocracy or influential *Veche* town councils. Suzdalia was, in fact, the birthplace of Russian autocracy and of the so-called 'appanage system' which was widely (though unjustly) blamed for Russia's collapse before the Mongol onslaught. This system of government and military organization was based upon a relationship between the Grand Prince of Suzdalia and surrounding princes, great and small, who were all members of the same ruling family. Authority tended to pass horizontally from brother to younger brother rather than vertically from father to son. To avoid excessive competition, the sons of princes who died before their father or elder brother were placed outside this succession system. It did not always work smoothly, but more often than not princes sent their *Druzhinas* to support threatened colleagues, while those on the frontiers received military assistance from the Grand Prince.

The northern principality of Polotsk was now outside the Kievan system and was already under threat from Lithuanian raiders. But the most

Mail shirts from forts west of Kiev, 12th-early 13th C; measurements in centimetres. Note the off-set opening in the 'standing' collar of the lower example. (Historical Museum, Zhitomir)

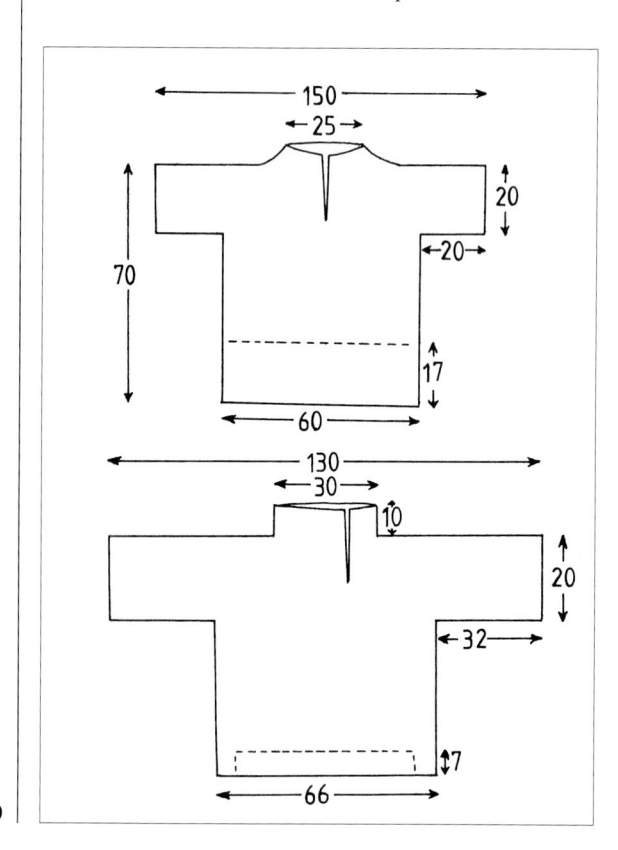

notable feature of northern Russia was the increasing independence of Novgorod, despite that city's inability to deal with major foreign invasions without help from one of the great princes. Novgorod was, in fact, the only Russian state which was not a principality. Instead it recognized the authority of the Grand Prince while its own bishop was titular head of state. In reality the *Veche* council governed the city and its vast dependent territories. Since the 12th century the *posadnik* governor had also been selected by the *Veche* from amongst Novgorod's own *boyar* aristocracy rather than by the Grand Prince. Furthermore the *Veche* now selected the bishop, the keeper of the treasury, the lord of state lands, various other officials including the *tysiatsky* militia commander, and sent its own *posadnik* to govern the *prisgorod* or 'dependent town' of Pskov.

Novgorod was, however, threatened by Baltic Crusaders and Lithuanian raiders, and opinion in the city was divided over how to deal with these Westerners. A pro-German faction emerged but would soon clash with those who prefered the tolerant rule of the Mongols to domination by Catholics. Similar tension would appear in Galich-Volhynia between those seeking alliances with Catholic Poland or pagan Lithuania and those willing to submit to the Mongols.

Although an expedition sent to crush tribes around the Pechora river in 1193 resulted in an appalling defeat from which only 80 men returned, Novgorod had expanded enormously to the north-east, causing further tensions with Suzdal-Vladimir. Meanwhile in the very far north, around the White Sea, Novgorod faced no threat to its domination despite occasional clashes between Russian and Norwegian fishermen.

Scale cuirass with iron elements attached to a soft leather base, 13th–14th centuries. (State Historical Museum, Moscow)

A Doomed Resistance: The Mongol Invasions

The Rus' did not heed the warnings of the first Mongol raids and as a result the Mongol invasion of Russia in 1237-39 came as a surprise, particularly as the enemy entered through dense forests to strike the principality of Ryazan. For their part the Mongols were no longer a nomad horde, and the Rus' now faced a Sino-Mongol army which drew upon the advanced military sciences of China as well as the warlike traditions of Central Asia. To this they found no answer. The Mongol Great Khan unleashed a campaign of terror to break the Rus' will to resist; Mongol armies maintained the field through all seasons, while Mongol siege methods drew heavily upon Chinese skills and specialists. In the end Prince Mikhail Vsevolodovich of Chernigov, brother of the better-known Alexander Nevski and the last Russian prince to submit to Mongols, made his way to the Great Khan's court in 1246. There he was executed, and was later declared a martyr-saint by the Russian Church.

An accomodation with the Mongols was the only realistic alternative, and the closeness of the subsequent relations between Grand Prince Alexander Nevski and his Mongol Great Khan overlord embarrassed

Russian chroniclers. On the other hand, a tradition of co-operation between the westernmost Russian principalities and their European neighbours also survived. Here Novgorod escaped prolonged Mongol control, while much of Belarus, Volhynia and Galich gradually fell under Lithuanian and Polish domination rather than that of the Mongols.

FURTHER READING

Anon., 'La Geste du Prince Igor', H.Grégoire, R.Jakobson & M.Szeftet (edit. & trans.), *Annuaire de l'Institut de Philologie et d'Histoire Orientale et Slaves* VIII (1945-47)

Anon., *The Chronicle of Novgorod: 1016-1471*, R.Michell & N.Forbes (trans.), *Camden Third Series, Vol.XXV* (London 1914)

Chadwick, N.K., *The Beginnings of Russian History* (Cambridge 1946)

Cherniavsky, M., *Tsar and People, Studies in Russian Myths* (New Haven 1961)

Dimnik, M., *Mikhail, Prince of Chernigov and Grand Prince of Kiev 1224-1246* (Toronto 1981)

Dukes, P., *A History of Russia: Medieval, Modern, Contemporary* (London 1974)

Fennell, J., *The Crisis of Medieval Russia 1200-1304* (London 1983)

Franklin, S. & J.Shepard, *The Emergence of Rus 750-1200* (London 1996)

Gimbutas, M., *The Slavs* (London 1971)

Grekov, B., *Kiev Rus* (Moscow 1959)

Gultzgoff, V., 'La Russie Kiévienne entre la Scandinavie, Constantinople et le Royaume Franc de Jérusalem', *Revue des Etudes Slaves* LV (1983), 151-161

Hannestad, K.(edit.), *Varangian Problems, Scando-Slavica, Supplementa I* (Copenhagen 1970)

Kaplan, F.I., 'The Decline of the Khazars and the Rise of the Varangians', *The American Slavic and East European Review* XIII (1954), 1-10

Kirpinikov, A.N., *Drevnerusskoi Oruzhye (Les Armes de la Russie Médiévale)*, in Russian with French summary (Leningrad 1971)

Kirpinikov, A.N., 'Russische Helm aus dem frühen Mittelalter', *Zeitschrift für Historische Waffen- und Kostümkunde* XV (1973), 89-98

Kirpinikov, A.N., 'Russische Körper-Schutzwaffen des 9.-16. Jahrhunderts', *Zeitschrift für Historische Waffen- und Kostümkunde* XVIII (1976), 22-37

Kirpinikov, A.N., 'Russische Waffen des 9.-15. Jahrhunderts', *Zeitschrift für Historische Waffen- und Kostümkunde* XXVIII (1986), 1-22

Kirpinikov, A.N., *Snaryazhenie Vsadnika I Verkhovogo Konya na Rusi, IX-XIIIbb (Harnachement du Cavalier et de la Monture en Russie aux IX-XIII siècles)*, in Russian with French summary (Leningrad 1973)

Kostochkin, V.,(edit.), *Krepostnoe Zodchestvo Drevniye Rusi (Fortress Architecture of Early Russia)*, in Russian with English summary (Moscow n.d.)

Lantzeff, G.V., & R.A.Pierce, *Eastward to Empire: Exploration and Conquest on the Russian Open Frontier, to 1750* (Montreal & London 1973)

Martin, J., 'Russian Expansion in the Far North, X to mid-XVI century', in M.Rywkin (edit.), *Russian Colonial Expansion to 1917* (London 1983), 23-43

(A) Knife blade from fortified monastery of St.Novikh, 9th-10th C
(B) Knife with wooden handle from grave near Zhovtnevoe, 8th-10th C
(C) Axehead from Novgorod, 9th C (Kremlin Museum, Novgorod)
(D) Axehead from Starya Ladoga, 9th-10th C
(E) Spearhead from Novgorod, 10th-13th C (Kremlin Museum, Novgorod)
(F-H) Spear and javelin heads from Starya Ladoga, 9th-10th C
(I) Spearhead from Gnezdovo, late 9th C (State Historical Museum, Moscow)
(J) Silver-plated mace from Tagantscha, 10th C
(K) Infantry war-axe from southern Russia, 10th-11th C
(L) Cavalry war-axe from southern Russia, 10th C
(M) War-axe inlaid with silver, Russian, 11th-13th C
(N) Silver inlaid war-axe from grave of Andrei Bogoljubskij, 12th C (National Historical Museum, Moscow)
(O) Fragments of shield from a Chernye Klobuki grave at Yureva near Ros river, 11th-13th C – O1, boss as found with fragments of rim reinforcement; O2, boss from front; O3, boss from side.
(P) Mace head from Kiev, 13th C
(Q) Mace head from Novgorod, 13thC (Kremlin Museum, Novgorod)
(R) Mace with replica haft, 12th-13th C
(S-U) Spearheads and spearbutt from Suzdal, 13th C (Historical Museum, Suzdal).

Martin, J., *Medieval Russia 980-1584* (Cambridge 1995)

Miller, D.B., 'The Many Frontiers of Pre-Mongol Rus', *Russian History* XIX (1992), 231-260

Noonan, T.S., 'Medieval Russia, the Mongols, and the West: Novgorod's relations with the Baltic, 1100-1350', *Medieval Studies* XXXVII (1975) 316-339.

Paszkiewicz, H., *The Origin of Russia* (London 1954)

Pritsak, O., *The Origins of Rus': Volume One, Old Scandinavian Sources other than Sagas* (Cambridge Mass. 1981)

Rappoport, P., 'Russian Medieval Military Architecture', *Gladius* VIII (1969), 39-62

Shepard, J., 'The Russian-Steppe frontier', in A. Bryer (edit.), *Byzantine Black Sea Symposium, Birmingham University 18-20 March 1978)* (Athens 1978), 123-133

Shepard, J., 'Yngvar's Expedition to the East and a Russian Inscribed Cross', *Saga-Book of the Viking Society* XXI (1982-85), 222-292

Thompson, M.W., *Novgorod the Great* (London 1967)

Topochko (et al., edits.), *Zemli Yuzhnoi Rusi v IX-XIVbb.*, Lands of the Southern Rus in the 9th-14th centuries (in Russian) (Kiev 1985)

Vernadsky, G., *A History of Russia*, Vols.II & III (New Haven 1948 & 1953)

Vernadsky, G., *The Origins of Russia* (Oxford 1959)

Ward, G.F., 'The English Danegeld and the Russian Dan', *The American and Slavic and East European Review* XIII (1954), 299-318

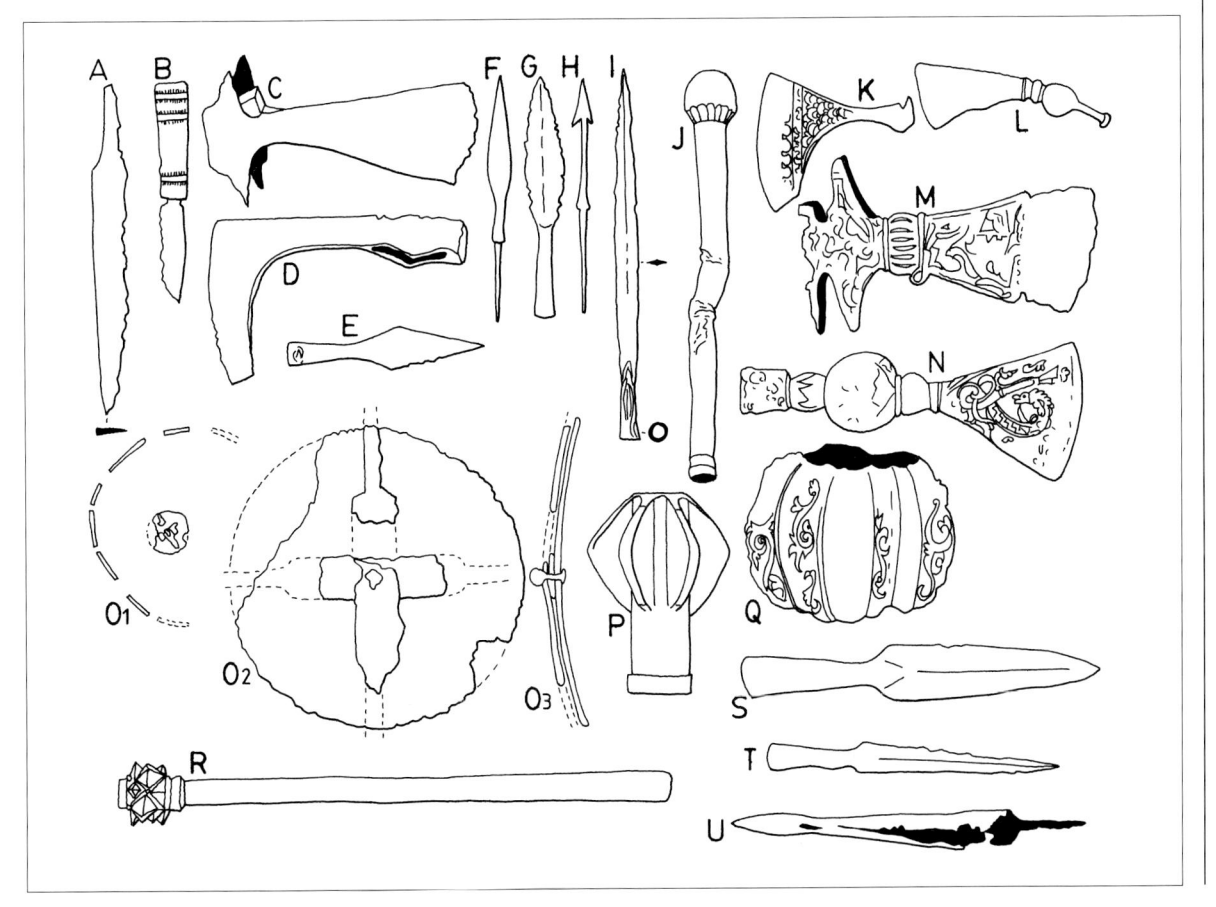

THE PLATES

PLATE A: BEFORE THE RUS', 9th CENTURY AD

The Scandinavian traders, adventurers and mercenaries who made their way ever deeper into the eastern Slav lands which were to become Russia did not fight their way through hostile territory. They must have had at least the grudging acceptance of local Slav tribesmen. When they reached the lands of the Turkish Khazars in the south, however, they entered the territory of an established state. Here the Khazar garrisons probably regarded these ferocious newcomers with suspicion.

A1: Eastern Slav tribal warrior

Archaeological evidence shows that the early Slavs were under greater steppe than Western European influence in military equipment, horse-harness and clothing. This warrior's lamellar cuirass is purely Central Asian in style, while his doubled-breasted coat looks Turkish. His ornamented belt has, however, been taken from a Finno-Ugrian foe. (Main sources: Slav & Eastern Finn grave-finds; Hermitage Museum, St.Petersburg; Historical Museums, Suzdal & Vladimir)

A2: Scandinavian merchant-venturer

At this early date Scandinavian settlers in Russia used weaponry either made in Scandinavia or manufactured locally in Scandinavian style. Arab travellers in Russia also described the Scandinavian-style quilted clothing and flowing cloaks of those they knew as Rus'. Early Rus' paganism is shown in this man's dagger with grip carved in the shape of Odin's Raven. (Main sources: shield from Gokstad ship burial, early 9th C, Universitetets Oldsaksamling, Oslo; axe, 9th-10th C, National Museum, inv.9798, Helsinki; helmet from Lermond, 10th century, Archaeological Museum, Oslo; dagger, 9th C, private collection)

A3: Eastern Magyar cavalryman

The advanced metallurgy of the Khazars and their Magyar allies is shown in many archaeological excavations, few of which are widely known outside Russia. In addition to helmets, mail hauberks and lamellar cuirasses, some of the Khazar-Magyar military elite wore plated leg and shoulder pieces reflecting Persian and Middle Eastern influence. It would be many centuries before such advanced armour was again seen in Europe. (Main sources: helmet, 9th-10th C, Hermitage Museum, St.Petersburg; armour & archery equipment from Cir-Jurt & arm defences from Borisov'skij, location unknown; leg defences from Gendjik-Tuapse, National Historical Museum, Moscow)

PLATE B: THE FIRST RUS', 9th-10th CENTURY

The first Rus' rulers of Kiev were pagans, and they tried to use existing pagan beliefs to weld the varied peoples of their sprawling realm into a unified state. But unsuccessful

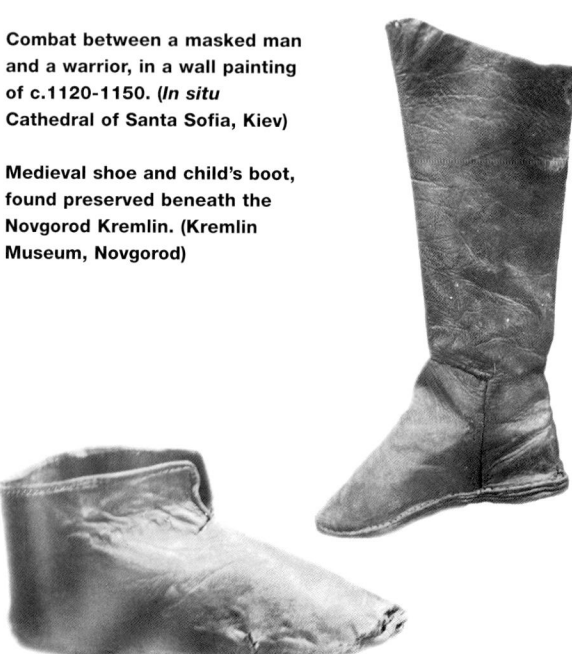

Combat between a masked man and a warrior, in a wall painting of c.1120-1150. (*In situ* Cathedral of Santa Sofia, Kiev)

Medieval shoe and child's boot, found preserved beneath the Novgorod Kremlin. (Kremlin Museum, Novgorod)

attacks on the powerful and wealthy Christian empire of Byzantium, like that attempted by Sviatoslav, probably convinced his successors that the Christian God would be a more effective ally than the old pagan pantheon.

B1: Sviatoslav of Kiev, 971 AD

Byzantine chroniclers described this early Rus' ruler as having shaved his head except for one long lock behind his ear; he was reportedly of middle height with a whispy beard, straggling moustache and snub nose. He wore the same white tunic as his followers, though his was cleaner. Clearly Sviatoslav was projecting himself as a steppe khan rather than a Viking adventurer or Byzantine emperor. (Main sources: carved drinking horn from Chernigov, 8th-9th C, National Historical Museum, Moscow; sword from Blistova, 9th-10th C, location unknown)

B2: Druzhina warrior of pagan Rus', 10th century
It did not take the Scandinavian Rus' long to adopt Slav and Turkish steppe clothing, arms and armour. Nevertheless there was a transitional phase when members of the *Druzhinas* used a mixture of North European and steppe weaponry. For example this warrior's sword is in Scandinavian form but with a locally made bronze hilt, whereas his archery equipment is essentially Central Asian, and his two-piece helmet is in Romano-Byzantine style. (Main sources: helmet from Gnezdovo, 10th C, National Historical Musuem, Moscow; armour from Chernaja Mogila, 10th C, National Historical Museum, Moscow; sword from Foscevataja, location unknown)

B3: Pecheneg chieftain, 10th-early 11th century
The little that is known of Pecheneg military equipment suggests that they did not differ much from nomads to the east, and that only a small elite had much armour. This warrior is from that elite, with a one-piece iron helmet perhaps of Middle Eastern origin, plus a mail hauberk over a quilted tunic. His weaponry and horse-harness include some distinctive Pecheneg decorative elements. (Main sources: gold ewer from Nagyszentmiklos, Khazar-Magyar, 10th C, Kunsthistorisches Museum, Vienna; sabre from Kursk area, 9th-13th C, State Anthropological Museum, Moscow; bridle from Gayevka, Hermitage Museum, St.Petersburg; helmet from Verkhne-Yichenkov, 11th C, Historical Museum, Rostov-on-Don)

PLATE C: WARRIORS OF KIEV, LATE 10th-11th CENTURY

Medieval Russia was a land of vast forests, particularly in the north and east; here rivers and lakes provided the only really effective routes. Unsurprisingly, the Rus' combined the ship-building heritage of their Scandinavian ancestors with the river-boat technology of the eastern Slavs, Finns, and forest Turks. Once the great rivers had been mastered the Rus' could become rulers of a region half the size of Europe.

C1: Commander of a princely army, 11th century
Byzantine military influence followed immediately the Rus' converted to Orthodox Christianity. Yet the main external influences remained those of steppe cultures and, later, of Western Europe. This senior commander still has the baggy eastern Slav trousers, a decorated helmet of steppe style, a Turkic sabre and an Iranian form of light cavalry axe. (Main sources: mace or staff of office from Tagantscha, 10th C, location unknown; helmet from Gnezdovo, 10th C, State Historical Musuem, Moscow; mail hauberk from Chernaja Mogila, State Historical Museum, Moscow)

C2: Member of a senior Druzhina of Kiev, 11th century
Byzantine influence is more obvious in this young warrior from a richly equipped *Druzhina*; yet he is based on artistic rather than archaeological evidence. His helmet and sword are genuine enough, but it is unclear when medieval Russian *Druzhinas* adopted kite-shaped shields. The pseudo-Roman hardened leather shoulder and waist extensions on his cuirass may have been an artistic convention. (Main sources: relief carvings of Sts. Nestor & Dimitri, 11th C, *in situ* Dimitriskaya, Kiev; sword-hilt from Kamenez-Podolsk, early 11th C, location unknown; helmet from Chernigov, mid-10th C, State Historical Museum, Moscow)

C3: Urban militiaman, 11th century
The majority of urban militias were poorly equipped, though this man's decorated axe suggests that he was wealthy if not necessarily warlike. The militias' main role was defensive, though merchants with experience of foreign lands served as guides. (Main sources: relief carving of man with shield from Kiev, 11th C, State Historical Museum, Moscow; war-axe, 11th-12th C, State Historical Museum, Moscow)

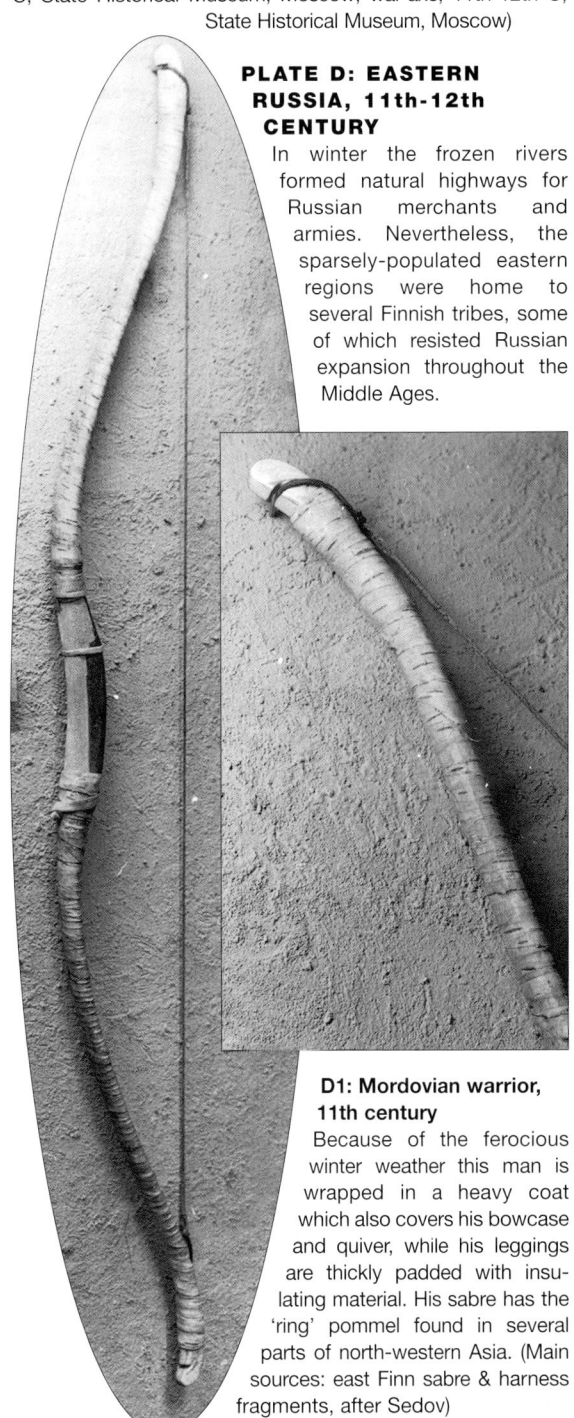

PLATE D: EASTERN RUSSIA, 11th-12th CENTURY

In winter the frozen rivers formed natural highways for Russian merchants and armies. Nevertheless, the sparsely-populated eastern regions were home to several Finnish tribes, some of which resisted Russian expansion throughout the Middle Ages.

D1: Mordovian warrior, 11th century
Because of the ferocious winter weather this man is wrapped in a heavy coat which also covers his bowcase and quiver, while his leggings are thickly padded with insulating material. His sabre has the 'ring' pommel found in several parts of north-western Asia. (Main sources: east Finn sabre & harness fragments, after Sedov)

Replica of a 12th century two-wood bow found near Novgorod, almost two metres long and covered in birchbark – see Plate D3. (Kremlin Museum, Novgorod)

Short-sleeved mail shirt, southern Rus' or Chernye Klobuki, 10th-13th century – see Plate E. (National Historical Museum, Moscow).

D2: Boyar nobleman, 11th-12th century
Even the wealth of Rus' principalities and their well-armed *Druzhinas* did not make their conquest of primitive and scattered neighbours easy. Those who led tribute-gathering expeditions could hope for rich rewards but needed to be well prepared. This *boyar* has an advanced form of lamellar cuirass plus the short-sleeved mail hauberk preferred by Russian warriors. (Main sources: saddle fragments from Lenkovtsi, Grodno & Belaya Vezha, 11th-12th C, location unknown; armour fragments from Novgorod, 11th-12th C, Kremlin Museum, Novgorod; bridle from Nikolaevka, 11th-12th C, Hermitage Museum, St.Petersburg; 'Sabre of Charlemagne', 11th C, Kunsthistoriches Museum, Vienna)

D3: Novgorod militiaman, 11th-12th century
Amongst several objects preserved in the waterlogged soil of northern Russia are a large bow of multiple wood construction, a pair of skis and a sledge. The bow was covered in birchbark, a material also used for sword-grips, shoes, quivers and writing 'paper'. This man's helmet came from a Lithuanian site but was probably made in northern Russia. (Main sources: skis, 13th-14th C, sword from Novgorod, 11th-12th C, bow from Novgorod region, 11th-12th C, all in Kremlin Museum, Novgorod)

PLATE E: SOUTHERN RUSSIA, 12th CENTURY
Southern Russia and the great city of Kiev were the cultural centre of the huge but increasingly fragmented kingdom of Rus'. Here an exotic mixture of Byzantine splendour, Slav and Turkish arms and armour, and Scandinavian traditions could be found. In our imagined scene, the little son of a *boyar* nobleman dares to offer his toy sword in homage to a great prince.

E1: Grand Prince of Kiev
Byzantine influence was unmistakable in the Palace of Kiev, where ceremonial regalia were modelled upon those of the Imperial Court in Constantinople. Even so Rus' princes continued to be portrayed wearing the fur hats which later became a mark of high rank in Rus' society. (Main sources: wall-painting, *in situ* Kiriilovskaya Monastery, 12th C, Kiev)

E2: Guardsman of the Grand Prince
Archaeology shows that actual arms and armour were not the same as those shown in most Byzantine-style pictures. How-ever, so few examples of Byzantine arms and armour survive that guards in Constantinople may have looked similar to this Rus' guardsman, who is based on a mixture of archaeological and pictorial evidence. (Main sources: wall-paintings, 1113-25 AD, *in situ* Cathedral of S.Sofia, Kiev; wall-paintings, mid-12th C, *in situ*, Monastery of Spaso Mirozhskaya, Kiev; helmet from Tagantscha, 12th-early 13th C, lost during World War Two; 'Axe of Andrei Bogoljubskij' & fragments of a cuirass from Kitaev, 12th-13th C, State Historical Museum, Moscow)

E3 & E4: Noblewoman and child
Russian female costume was similar to that of Byzantium and not so very different from that of the rest of Europe. In almost all medieval societies children's clothing was a smaller version of that worn by their elders, and the same was true of the Rus'. The wooden toy sword was found during excavations of medieval Novgorod. (Main sources: manuscript painting of 'Grand Duke Sviatoslav Yaroslavich and his family' in the *Izbornik Sviatoslav*, 1073 AD, State Historical Museum, Moscow; wooden toy swords, Kremlin Museum, Novgorod)

PLATE F: NORTHERN & EASTERN RUSSIA, 12th CENTURY
While Kievan Rus' tore itself apart in civil wars, the merchant city-state of Novgorod got on with the business of creating its own 'fur empire' in the far north. This entailed maintaining tiny *pogost* trading and administrative outposts across vast

stretches of the inhospitable terrain – though the difficulties came mainly from the weather rather than from the scattered indigenous peoples. Monks probably played a vital role in maintaining communications, perhaps delivering the birchbark documents which were used instead of paper.

F1: Russian monk
As elsewhere in the Orthodox Church, monks wore simple black habits and long beards. This man carries government documents written on rolls of birchbark, and his shoes are also made of this material – *bast*.

F2: Posadnik governor
By the 12th century Russian male costume had developed its own distinctive characteristics, having much in common with those of the Turco-Islamic world. It was distinguished from Byzantine costume by greater use of furs. (Main sources: bridle from Chernavino, 11th-early 12th C, Hermitage Museum, St.Petersburg; stirrups from Knezha Gora, 12th-early 13th C, Historical Museum, Kiev; saddle fragments from Zelenki, 12th-13th C, Hermitage Museum, St.Petersburg; helmet visor, 12th C, & iron mace head, 12th-13th C, locations unknown)

F3: Garrison soldier
Since this man is employed by one of the northern Rus' states his arms and armour are similar to those used in Poland or Scandinavia, particularly his simple helmet of two-piece construction and kite-shaped shield. The sword is of a type seen among neighbouring Baltic peoples, while the dagger is particularly Russian. (Main sources: carved wooden panel showing warriors, Novgorod, 12th C, & leather sheath, Novgorod, 12th-13th C, Kremlin Museum, Novgorod; inlaid metal object, 12th C, Historical Museum, Pskov; sword from Livonia, 11th-12th C, Latvian National Museum, Riga)

G: THE CHERNYE KLOBUKI, 12th – EARLY 13th CENTURY
Medieval Russia was constantly trying to expand from the forests and forested steppe regions into the true steppes of the south and south-east. Here, however, they came up against Turkish and latterly Mongol states whose armies were far more effective on these open grasslands. Their most valuable steppe allies were the *Chernye Klobucki*, the so-called 'Black Hoods'.

G1: Russian noble warrior
Relations between the *Chernye Klobuki* and Rus' ruling classes were close. Mutual influence between their military equipment is seen in the short mail hauberk and new form of cuirass worn by this Russian *boyar*. His helmet, weaponry and horse-harness are, however, more European. (Main sources: inlaid spearhead from Chernigov, early 13th C, & lamellar fragments from Zaytsevskoye, 12th-13th C, locations unknown; helmet from Moscu, 12th-13th C, National Historical Museum, Bucharest; spurs & stirrup from Knezha Gora, 12th-early 13th C, Historical Museum, Kiev)

G2: Senior member of Chernye Klobuki
The main feature which distinguishes this 'Black Hood' leader from the *boyar* is his archery equipment and lighter armour. He uses a whip rather than spurs, rides with shorter stirrups, and wears a helmet of Asiatic form. (Main sources: belt from Voinesti, 12th-13th C, National Historical Museum, Bucharest; spearhead from Burti, 12th C, & mail hauberk from Kovali, 12th-13th C, State Historical Museum, Moscow; helmet from Babiche, late 12th-early 13th C, Hermitage

Sabre; spired, fluted helmet with mask visor; and mail shirt (note configuration at neck – and deep slits up from hem front and back, indicating cavalry use). All early 13th century, Chernye Klobuki. (Hermitage Museum, St.Petersburg)

Museum, St.Petersburg; harness from Gayevka, 12th-13th C, location unknown)

G3: Chernye Klobuki standard-bearer
A number of very distinctive tall, fluted helmets with iron face-masks have been found in southern and eastern Russia as well as Byzantine Constantinople. Quite where this style originated is still a matter of debate, though it would later be associated with the Mongols and Tatars. As a standard-bearer this man probably has a lamellar cuirass beneath his decorated tunic. The banner, with an image of St.George, is based on a Russian icon. (Main sources: helmet, face-mask & sabre from Kovali, 12th-13th C, State Historical Museum, Moscow; tunic from Cingul Kurgan with decorative fabric altered, 13th C, Historical Museum, Kiev; spear-blade & butt, 13th C, Historical Museum, Suzdal)

47

PLATE H: FACING THE MONGOLS, EARLY 13th CENTURY

The armies of 13th century Russia were sophisticated, well equipped, and drew on several different military traditions – European, Turkish/steppe nomadic, Byzantine, and perhaps even Islamic Persian. When the Mongols burst upon the scene, however, the Russians found themselves up against something new. Here was an invader who was not only more united and disciplined, more mobile and self-sufficient, but one who could draw upon the advanced military technology of China.

H1: Boyar from Galich

The military elite of Galich and to some extent Volhynia were armed in a similar manner to Hungarians and Poles, giving them a more European appearance than troops from Kiev or Suzdal. Nevertheless their basic armour was old-fashioned compared to that of Germany, France or even Scandinavia. The massive heated crossbow bolt which has pierced his shield was one of many unpleasant technological shocks introduced by the Mongols. (Main sources: sword & scabbard of Prince Daumantas, mid-13th C, Historical Museum, Pskov; gold-inlaid bronze doors, 13th C, in situ Cathedral, Suzdal; helmet of Yaroslav Vsevolodovich, mid-13th C, Kremlin Armoury, Moscow)

H2: Volhynian militia crossbowman

The tall, brimmed war-hat may have been of Chinese origin but spread westwards before the Mongols; few examples survive, and one of the simplest has been given to this crossbowman from western Rus'. Beneath a mail hauberk his tunic is distinctly Russian, though his crossbow is identical to those used elsewhere in Europe. (Main sources: helmet from western Russia, 12th-13th C, Historical Museum, Kiev; lead seals, Russia, mid-13th C, location unknown; crossbow equipment from Novgorod, mid-13th C, Hermitage Museum, St.Petersburg)

H3: Lithuanian warrior

Being pagans, the Lithuanian warrior class still buried their dead with arms, armour and utensils for the afterlife. Much of this was imported from east or west, yet the final assembly remained distinctively Lithuanian. The lower legs, obscured here, are wound with puttees. (Main sources: helmet & sword from Prussia, belt from Livonia, 11th-13th C, after Sedov)

INDEX

(References to illustrations are shown in **bold**. Plates are prefixed 'pl.' with commentary locators in brackets, e.g. 'pl. **D3** (46)')

Alexander Nevski 8, 41
archery 20, 33, 34, 35-36, 45 (D1)
  ill: pl. **A3** (44), **B2** (45), **D3** (46), **G2** (47); **7, 16, 45**

Balts **4**, 4, 5, 11, 36, 47 (F3)
birchbark: pl. **F1** (47); **16, 24, 45**, 46
blood vengeance 5, 14
boyars: pl. **D2** (46), **E3/4** (46), **G1** (47), **H1** (48); 15, 22, 24, 40, 41
Bulgars **4**, 5, 7, 8, 10, **12**, 16, 17, 24, 36, 37, 39
Byzantines **4**, 7-24 passim, **12**, 35-48 passim

cavalry *see* horsemen
Chernigov 8, **12**, 19, 22, 41
Chernye Klobuki ('Black Hoods') 7, 21-22, 33, 34, 35, 39, 40
  ill: pl. **G** (47); **12, 35, 43**, 46
children: pl. **E4** (46); 23, 34
commanders: pl. **C1** (45); 18, 19, 20, 37, 41
costume & equipment 13, 21, 24-34, 36
  misc ill: pl. **A-H** (44-48); **3, 5, 16, 24, 44**
  armour 5, 20, 33, 34
    pl. ill: **A-H** (44-48) passim
    other ill: **3, 24, 33, 34, 35, 40, 41, 46, 47**
  shields 22, 23, 33, 34, 37
    ill: pl. **A2** (44), **C2/3** (45), **F3** (47), **H1** (48); **3, 34, 43, 44**
  weaponry 19, 20, 22, 24, 33, 34, 35-36, 39
    pl. ill: **A-H** (44-48) passim
    other ill: **7, 16, 34, 36, 43, 44, 45, 47**

Druzhinas: pl. **B2** (45), **C2** (45); 18-19
  misc refs: 10-40 passim, 46

Finno-Ugrians: pl. **D** (45); 3-21 passim, **12**, 34, 35, 44, 45
fortifications 5, 6, 13, 15, 20, 21, 38-40
  ill: **6-23** passim, **38, 39**

Galich: pl. **H1** (48); 8, 9, **12**, 17, 24, 37, 39, 40-42
garrisons: pl. **F3** (47); 15, 17, 35, 39

hairstyles: pl. **B1** (44); 23, 24

Harald Hardrada 18
horsemen 5, 6, 14, 19, 21, 33, 34, 35, 36, 37
  horses & harness 20, 23, 33, 34, 36, 44 (A1)
  ill: pl. **A3** (44), **B3** (45), **D1** (45), **D2** (46), **F2** (47), **G** (47); **5, 7, 8, 16**
Hungarians 4-5, 8, **12**, 17, 21, 24, 40, 48 (H1)
hunting **7, 8**, 19

Igor of Kiev 7, 10
Izgoi ('hired men') 19

Khagans 7, 9-10, 10-11, 15, 23, 24
Khazars 4-17 passim, **4, 5**, 33, 38, 44 (A)
  ill: pl. **B** (44-45), **C** (45), **E** (46); **4, 12, 15**
Kiev/Kievan Rus' 4-13, 15-20, 37, 38, 39, 40
Kipchak Turks 5, 7, 8, **12**, 16, 17, 21-22, 37, 40

Lithuanians: pl. **H3** (48); 4, 9, **12**, **36**, 39, 40-42

Magyars: pl. **A3** (44); 4-5, 7, 10, 15, 33
Mikhail Vsevolodovich 41
militias: pl. **C3** (45), **D3** (46), **H2** (48); 15, 16, 17, 19-20, 37, 40, 41
Mongols 5, 8-9, 20, 22, 24, 33, 37, 40, 41-42, 47
monks: pl. **F1** (47); 23
Mordvians: pl. **D1** (45); 3, 4, 8, **12**

Novgorod 5-6, 7, 8, 9, 10, 16-17, 20, 21, 33, 39, 41, 42
  ill: pl. **D3** (46), **F** (46-47); **4, 12, 19, 20, 23**

Pechenegs: pl. **B3** (45); **4**, 5, 7, 10, 13, 16, 17, 21
Pereyaslavl **6**, 7, **12**, 17, 36, 38
Poles 7, **12**, 17, 18, 20, 21, 24, 40, 41, 42, 47 (F3), 48 (H1)
portages **4**, 10, 20, 34-35, 36
posadnik governors: pl. **F2** (47); 16, 19, 41
princes 15-16, 17, 18, 19, 20, 22, 33, 37, 40
  Grand Princes 15, 17, 21, 36, 37, 40, 41
  ill: pl. **B1** (44), **E1** (46); **22, 23, 33, 36**

religion 14-15, 17, 22-23
  Christianity: pl. **F1** (47); 7, 9, 15, 21, 22, 23, 40, 41, 45 (C1)

  saints: pl. **G3** (47); **3**, 14-15, **21**, 23, **24**, 33, **37, 38**, 41
    see also Alexander Nevski; Vladimir I
  Judaism 4, 15, 17
  paganism: pl. **A2** (44); 5, 11, 14-15, **18**, 23, 37, 41, 44 (B), 48 (H3)
rivers & rivercraft **3**, 7, 9, 10, 13, 14, 20, 22, 34-35, 36-37
  ill: pl. **C** (45); **4, 12**
  ushkuynik river pirates 16, 34
Rostov 17, 36, 39
Rurik 7, 9, 10, 16, 40
Rus' 3, 4, 5, 6, 7, 8, 9-20, 21, 22-42
  ill: pl. **A2** (44), **B/C** (44-45), **D2/3** (46), **E/F** (46-47), **G1** (47); **4, 12**

Scandinavians: pl. **A2** (44); 6, 7, 8, 9, 10-11, 15-33 passim, 38, 45, 47
Seljuk Turks **12**, 17, 18
siege warfare 19, 39, 41
slaves 15, 22
Slavs: pl. **A1** (44); 3-40 passim, 45, 46
Starya Ladoga **4, 5**, 7, 9, 10, **12, 38**, 38
Suzdal/ia 8, **11, 12**, 17, 34, 36, 37, 39, 40, 41, 48 (H1)
Sviatoslav of Kiev: pl. **B1** (44); 13, 24

tactics 33, 35-37
tribal levies (*Voi*) 13, 16, 20
tribute-gathering 10, 16-17, 19, 38, 46
Turks 5, 7, 8, 9, 15-40 passim, 45, 46, 47, 48

Varjazi/Varangians 11, 13, 14, 18, 24, 33, 35
Veche town councils 16, 17, 20, 40, 41
Vladimir I: 7, 11, 14, 15, 16, 38, 39
Vladimir (principality) 8-9, **12, 17**, 17, **18**, 41
Volhynia: pl. **H2** (48); 4, 9, **12**, 37, 39, 40, 41, 42, 48 (H1)

waggons 34, 37
women: pl. **E3** (46); 5, 15

Yaroslav I (the Wise) 15, 18, 37, 39
Yaroslav Vsevolodovich **23, 33**, 48 (H1)